Nurturing Hope

Nurturing Hope

Christian Pastoral Care
in the Twenty-First Century

Lynne M. Baab

NURTURING HOPE
Christian Pastoral Care in the Twenty-First Century

All biblical references in this book come from the New Revised Standard Version, unless otherwise noted.

All stories of individuals are told with permission. Names of individuals and congregations have been changed to respect privacy.

Cover and interior design: Rob Dewey
Typesetting: PerfecType, Nashville, TN

Print ISBN: 978-1-5064-3427-8
eBook ISBN: 978-1-5064-3428-5

The paper used in this publication meets the minimum requirements of American National Standard for Information Sciences — Permanence of Paper for Printed Library Materials, ANSI Z329.48-1984.

Manufactured in the U.S.A.

Contents

Series Preface

MY MOST sincere wish is that the Living with Hope series will offer comfort, wisdom—and hope—to individuals facing life's most common and intimate challenges. Books in the series tackle complex problems such as addiction, parenting, unemployment, pregnancy loss, serious illness, trauma, and grief and encourage individuals, their families, and those who care for them. The series is bound together by a common message for those who are dealing with significant issues: you are not alone. There is hope.

This series offers first-person perspectives and insights from authors who know personally what it is like to face these struggles. As companions and guides, series contributors share personal experiences, offer valuable research from trusted experts, and suggest questions to help readers process their own responses and explore possible next steps. With empathy and honesty, these accessible volumes reassure individuals they are not alone in their pain, fear, or confusion.

The series is also a valuable resource for pastoral and spiritual care providers in faith-based settings. Parish pastors, lay ministers, chaplains, counselors, and other staff and volunteers can draw on these volumes to offer skilled and compassionate guidance to individuals in need of hope.

Each title in this series is offered with prayer for the reader's journey—one of discovery, further challenges, and transformation. You are not alone. There is hope.

Beth Ann Gaede, Series Editor

Titles in the Living with Hope Series

Nurturing Hope: Christian Pastoral Care in the Twenty-First Century
(Lynne M. Baab)

*Dignity and Grace: Wisdom for Caregivers and Those Living with
Dementia* (Janet L. Ramsey)

Jobs Lost, Faith Found: A Spiritual Resource for the Unemployed
(Mary C. Lindberg)

*They Don't Come with Instructions: Cries, Wisdom, and Hope for
Parenting Children with Developmental Challenges*
(Hollie M. Holt-Woehl)

True Connection: Using the NAME IT Model to Heal Relationships
(George Faller and Heather P. Wright)

Waiting for Good News: Living with Chronic and Serious Illness
(Sally L. Wilke)

Acknowledgments

I COULD not have written the first half of this book without
the syllabus prepared by Lydia Fuller Johnson for Perspectives
on Pastoral Care, which she taught in 2014 at the University of
Otago in Dunedin, New Zealand. Lydia said that if she could have
subtitled the course, it would have been "The Changing Face of
Pastoral Care." I used Lydia's material in 2016 to teach the course.
Throughout the semester, I was so grateful for the informative
readings she chose, many of which are quoted in this book, and
her deep understanding of trends in pastoral care. Lydia's syllabus
contributed so much to the first half of this book, and she also
clarified several issues for me while I was writing it. Thank you,
Lydia, for sharing your depth of knowledge so generously.

I also could not have written this book without my students,
particularly in the classes I taught at the University of Otago on
chaplaincy, missional church, ministry in a culturally diverse society,
and pastoral care. I teach largely by discussion, and my students
have taught me so much as they have recounted stories about what
ministry today looks like in practice and as they have shared their
convictions. Thank you, students, for engaging so enthusiastically in
classroom discussions and in essays.

The material in the listening chapter was shaped by conversations
with Jayme Koerselman. People who clarified various points for me
include Murray Rae and Geoff Bevan. I am grateful for their help.

The three spiritual directors I have seen over the past twenty years
modeled effective listening and pastoral care that empowers. Thank
you, Kathleen Fischer, Catherine Fransson, and Sister Judith Anne
O'Sullivan, for the many ways you influenced and grounded me in
Christ. I also want to thank two psychotherapists, Susan Snyder and

John Farnsworth, for modeling deep listening and for giving me insight about wise living.

I am so grateful for the many friends and small-group members who cared for me during my sixteen years of depression and in the years when I was learning how to live as a nondepressed person. I can't even imagine what my life would be like today without the listening, support, and prayer I received in those hard years.

Over the past couple of decades, many people have told me their stories about being caregivers and care recipients, and those stories shaped this book. Warm thanks to my mother, Teddy Mitchell, as well as to Connie Anderson, Mike Baab, Anne Baumgartner, Dan Baumgartner, Lynne Blessing, Brenda Burnett, Dave Campbell, Debbie Campbell, Nancy Carlstrom, Julie Christensen, Linda Cutshall, Peter Dobbs, Helen Harray, Beth Hess, Patti Holman, Greg Hughson, Kimberlee Conway Ireton, Lisa Keosababian, Andy Karplus, Karen Karplus, Tom Larkin, Sylvia Lidell, Rose Luxford, Martin Macaulay, Sue Macaulay, Emma McPhail, Janet Moore, Sebastian Murrihy, Geoff New, Paddy Payne, Kelly Pearson, Jane Pelz, Susan Phillips, Christopher Ross, Dianne Ross, Margui Rutherford, Adrienne Scholsser-Hall, Sarah Sanderson, Carol Simon, Steve Simon, Renee Sundberg, Anne Thomson, Gill Trebilco, Margie Van Duzer, and Heather Wright.

I give special thanks to Chaplain Mike Wright, who profoundly shaped my understanding of the ministry of presence. Well done, good and faithful servant. Rest in peace.

Twenty years ago, when I got my first book contract, I was assigned a wonderful editor, Beth Gaede. Beth is the editor of this series, and we have now worked on six books together. Beth has challenged and encouraged me in so many ways. Thank you, Beth, for helping me to be a much better writer.

My husband, Dave Baab, has cared for me in just about every way described in this book. Dave, I can't thank you enough for your loving kindness to me and to our family members. Your love has upheld us.

Introduction

Christian Pastoral Care in the Twenty-First Century

RIGHT AFTER lunch on a sunny day in 1972, a minister began an afternoon filled with pastoral care appointments. First, he drove to the hospital and sat with a woman from his congregation for half an hour. They chatted about her abdominal surgery the day before, her hospital stay, and what would happen when she got home. He prayed with her.

Next, he drove to the home of a family who had just lost a son in Vietnam. He talked with the family about the grief process, and together they began to plan the funeral service. After that visit, the minister returned to his office, where he had an appointment with a man who had lost his job. They brainstormed options and connections for his job search and made an appointment to talk again the following week.

Several decades ago, these three activities—visiting someone with a medical problem, meeting with a family to talk about grief and plan a funeral, and offering pastoral counseling in the church office—made up the majority of what many Christians considered to be pastoral care. These tasks were viewed as the responsibility of the paid minister.

Much pastoral care centered on pastoral counseling, a psychological approach to human need. Care recipients were usually members of the congregation where the minister was employed. By the time the twenty-first century started, this pattern had already begun to shift.

With each passing year, the practice of pastoral care has changed
further.

What Is Pastoral Care Today?

The word "pastoral" in "pastoral care" comes from the Latin
pastoralis, which means "related to herdsmen or shepherds." The
historical understanding of pastoral care is rooted in the passages in
the Hebrew Scriptures and the New Testament about God as our
Shepherd, Jesus as our Good Shepherd, and the call to Christian
leaders to act like shepherds to the people under their care.
= problematic

The care that shepherds provide for sheep includes feeding,
guidance, protection, healing, and seeking out the lost. In
many congregations today, a significant amount of this kind of
shepherding happens in small groups, music teams, and various task
groups where the members provide care and support for each other.
For people in need who may not be connected to a small group or
task group, or who have very significant needs, pastoral care may be
provided by paid and unpaid ordained ministers, paid or unpaid lay
ministers, as well as other congregational leaders and members.

New
Care by various church groups, ministers, and members is given
both to congregation members and to people outside congregations.
Increasingly, pastoral care involves showing love across ethnic and
religious boundaries. In comparison with several decades ago, more
diverse people care for others in a pastoral way, and the settings for
pastoral care have greatly expanded.

Today we have a much greater understanding of the pitfalls of
pastoral care. The carer can become too invested in the needs of the
care recipient and morph into a rescuer rather than someone who
comes alongside. Carers can become so overwhelmed with people's
needs that they forget about self-care and stewardship of energy and
gifts.

Christian pastoral care must include a conscious awareness of God's
presence, empowerment, and healing. Christian carers nurture

Christian pastoral
care must include a
conscious awareness
of God's presence,
empowerment, and
healing.

Happy are those whose help is the God of Jacob,
whose hope is in the Lord their God,
who made heaven and earth,
the sea, and all that is in them;
who keeps faith for ever;
who executes justice for the oppressed;
who gives food to the hungry.

The Lord sets the prisoners free;
the Lord opens the eyes of the blind.
The Lord lifts up those who are bowed down.

—Psalm 146:5–8

others because God cares. Without this perspective, the whole endeavor of pastoral care is rooted solely in human strength and wisdom, and does not differ from the care and counseling provided by psychotherapists, school counselors, and employee assistance providers in the workplace. Pastoral care then becomes an exercise in human caring, which is not at all a bad thing in itself. However, today we are more aware that pastoral care by Christians must be grounded in an understanding of God as the true caregiver and healer, whether stated or unstated.

Pastoral Care Trends in Action

Leah's ministry illustrates some of these trends. For more than thirty years, Leah has served a midsized urban congregation as director of congregational care, working under seven senior pastors, both men and women. She keeps track of the pastoral care needs in the congregation, staying in conversation with the senior pastor and referring some of the people in need to them. She trains and oversees the lay pastoral care team, which meets many practical needs, like meals and help with moving.

The lay pastoral carers are trained to engage relationally as well as practically, and they feel confident, or grow in confidence, talking with and praying with people in need. Leah also oversees the welcome of newcomers, hosting newcomer gatherings six times a year and running classes for new members several times a year. These responsibilities have remained relatively constant over three decades, in part because her congregation was on the forefront of forming lay pastoral care teams when she began her work. Leah herself has a master's degree in Christian education and has not been ordained as a minister.

Despite the sense of continuity Leah experiences, sometimes she finds herself bemused at the many aspects of pastoral care that have changed. When she talks with congregation members who struggle with anxiety, she finds herself recommending a book on mindfulness meditation, a spiritual practice she had not heard of when she began her job. When people bemoan the tyranny of the smart-phone world, she often responds by talking about fasting—not fasting from food, but fasting from Facebook or other forms of social media.

People in their twenties and thirties talk with her about their desire to have less clutter in their homes and to feel less scattered in their daily lives. Leah tells them about the long-held Christian monastic tradition of simplicity and the peace that comes from it. She keeps a list of spiritual directors, because she often gets requests for referrals. Fasting, simplicity, and spiritual direction were seldom on the radar screen for most Protestants several decades ago.

Another change Leah has experienced is the increasing diversity in her congregation. Unlike many congregations where ethnic diversity is growing, Leah's congregation is located in an ethnically homogeneous neighborhood, and the congregation is mostly white. The congregation, however, has grown in socioeconomic diversity, and Leah and the lay pastoral care team have embraced the complex challenges of welcoming people who are dealing with economic hardship.

The members of the congregation are much more diverse in their faith backgrounds as well. The congregation's Alpha program,

In comparison with several decades ago, more diverse people care for others in a pastoral way, and the settings for pastoral care have greatly expanded.

which has run off and on for almost two decades, means that some members come from unchurched backgrounds. A large percentage of newer members come from other denominations, and Leah often finds herself explaining to newcomers how the leadership structures in her congregation work.

Many challenges today are similar to those from decades ago, such as job loss, health issues, death and mourning, and family complexities. However, Leah, like most people, has observed a rapid increase in societal change and challenges. Because the speed of change has increased, many people feel off-balance long before crisis hits and are therefore less resilient when new challenges arise. Effective and loving pastoral care is therefore more necessary now than ever.

Political polarization has created societal distrust, an underlying stressor that also reduces resilience. The rise of smart phones and the ever-present availability of the internet and social media have raised significant questions about what a good life looks like. Consumerism continues to ramp up, contributing to anxiety and economic stress. In this volume, I will discuss these and other stressors, as well as appropriate pastoral care in response to the great impact of stress on the body, mind, emotions, and spiritual well-being.

Purposes for Pastoral Care

What is the goal of pastoral care? To give aid in specific situations? To help people solve their problems? To lift burdens off the shoulders of individuals who are heavy laden with life's pain and responsibility? In the mid- to late twentieth century, the predominant model for pastoral care was pastoral counseling, based on psychotherapeutic models. Many ministers who were trained several decades ago are still deeply influenced by that model. While pastoral counseling remains significant in some settings today, many additional models for pastoral care have emerged. I have described some of those shifts already, and the chapters in the first half of this book will explore more models.

In the light of current trends, two writers have shaped my understanding of why and how Christians are called to engage in pastoral care today. These writers have provided helpful language to describe the significance of offering pastoral care from a uniquely Christian perspective. Pastoral care may involve physical help, discussion of practical needs, or exploration of emotions—all of which are aspects of shepherding—and the subject of God or faith may not come up at all in some pastoral care settings.

Christian pastoral care, however, is always grounded in the grace of God as shown in Jesus Christ, empowered by the Holy Spirit. Even though the first writer I'll mention, Nancy Tatom Ammerman, conducted research across many different religions, her conclusions have significant implications for Christians who want to engage in pastoral care that draws on God's love in Christ.

Ammerman is a sociologist of religion, and in 2013 I had the privilege of hearing her describe her recent research, which would be published a few months later in her book *Sacred Stories, Spiritual Tribes: Finding Religion in Everyday Life.*[1] She and her team of researchers interviewed dozens of people in two major cities, talking with them at length about their religious and spiritual commitments, in the broadest sense of those words. The interviewees included Protestants, Roman Catholics, Jews, Muslims, Hindus, Buddhists, atheists, and people committed to various forms of new age and pagan practices.

The researchers found that the people who had the deepest commitments to any form of spirituality—whether to a Buddhist meditation practice or the Christian faith—frequently talked with others about the implications of their spiritual practice or commitment in everyday life. Ammerman described the content of these conversations as the overlap of "the ordinary and the non-ordinary" or the intersection of the "sacred and the secular."[2]

These conversations allow participants to explore divine action in human life, to describe the implications of their faith in everyday life, or to talk about "something that calls us beyond ourselves."[3]

Christian pastoral care must include a conscious awareness of God's presence, empowerment, and healing. Christian carers provide nurture to others because God cares.

According to Ammerman's research, most people learn to talk about this intersection of the sacred and daily life in communities of faith, and these conversations take place most often in homes, workplaces, and congregations.[4]

Christians believe that God is present in all of life. In all situations, the God who was incarnate in Jesus Christ is already there, through the power of the Holy Spirit. We don't have to urge God to be present; Jesus promised to be with us always (Matt 28:20). When we talk about the intersection of daily life and Christian faith, or the overlap of the ordinary and the non-ordinary, we are simply acknowledging that while God is present in all of life, often we find it difficult to perceive God's presence and need help to do so.

Ammerman's research gave me a new understanding of what happens in many settings within congregations. For example, I had always seen small groups as a place for many good things: friendship, support, encouragement, Bible study, exploration of faith issues, and prayer with others. This research highlighted one more purpose and blessing of small groups: participants have the opportunity to talk about the overlaps of the Christian faith and their everyday life. God is already present, and the language of overlap or intersection helps us look for that presence.

Where is God when my teenager is off the rails? In what ways has God answered my prayers about her? In what ways has God given me peace about the situation and guided me to resources and support? Might I pray in new ways for her? People who will listen and draw me out as I explore these topics are providing pastoral care to me.

Caregivers wonder, "What shall I *say*?" "What can I *do*?" Yet these questions are secondary to our being a *presence*, a reminder of the Presence of God in Jesus Christ, that sufferers are not alone. We are sharers with them of their burdens as we fulfill the law of Christ (Galatians 6:2). Our own self-awareness of this "being with" them prompts us to give thanks that neither they nor we are alone; the Presence of God is with us, bearing the pain, agony and desolation with us.

—Wayne Oates, *Grief, Transition and Loss: A Pastor's Practical Guide*[5]

In addition to small groups, many other congregational settings make space for conversations where individuals are able to express connections between the sacred and ordinary events of their lives and listen to others help them consider new ways of seeing God at work in everyday life. These conversations happen when washing dishes after church dinners and when chatting in the parking lot after meetings. "I prayed for you last week about your job. What happened at work this week? Did you feel God's help with that difficult situation?"

Ammerman and her researchers found that the frequency of such conversations in Christian congregations was not correlated with any particular position on the theological spectrum. Instead, more conversations between faith and daily life took place in congregations that had more activities of any kind.[6] Quite simply, people talk about the impact of their faith on their everyday life whenever they gather with others in their congregation.

Therefore, providing opportunities for classes, seminars, musical rehearsals, arts events, working bees, mission projects, committees, and other activities makes space for people to talk about this overlap. Ammerman's research gave me language to describe this significant aspect of congregational life, one I had noticed all my adult life but had never singled out for attention. Christians get together for many reasons, and one significant reason—almost always unstated—is so we can talk about where we perceive God to be in everyday life.

Pastoral carers open up space to allow people to consider the overlap between their everyday life and what they believe and experience about God. Carers help people talk through the challenging situations of their life in the light of the ways God is already at work or ways they would like to see God at work. Beliefs rooted in the Bible—about God, Jesus, the Holy Spirit, the role of prayer, the significance of community, the meaning of family, and so on—have an impact on the way people view the situations they're in.

Pastoral carers listen to people talk about these connections, asking follow-up questions and telling occasional stories from their own

Christians get together for many reasons, and one significant reason—almost always unstated—is so we can talk about where we perceive God to be in everyday life.

life and the lives of others that provide new ideas about how to notice and understand the overlap.

In some settings, care receivers aren't ready to talk about the intersection of their faith and their daily life. Perhaps they don't have what they consider to be spiritual beliefs. In that instance the carer listens carefully and asks gentle questions about the care recipients' values and priorities in life. Perhaps care receivers are feeling confused about their faith or are struggling to find God anywhere in their life. The pastoral carer may then guide the conversation to a discussion about feelings of the absence of God.

In some settings, such as small groups and conversations in congregations, members participate in a back-and-forth conversational flow. In some moments, individuals are care receivers, talking about the connections between what they believe and how they live, thinking out loud about the issues. In other instances, those same individuals are caregivers, listening to others talk about connections and perhaps telling brief stories from their own life for the purpose of helping others rather than for themselves. This fluidity in roles—the willingness to receive care sometimes and give care other times—is a sign of maturity.

Ammerman's research uses the language of "overlap" and "intersection" to describe something significant that happens in conversations, an exploration of how a person's convictions about God, the Bible, prayer, the holy, the sacred, or other aspects of a faith commitment connect with daily life. Conversations about these topics play a central role in the practice of Christian pastoral care, and play a role in what was historically called "cure of souls."

Cure of Souls

Eugene Peterson, author of many books about pastoral leadership and translator of *The Message*, provides additional perspective on the purpose of pastoral care that has interesting connections with Ammerman's work. For several decades, Peterson has advocated a shift in pastors' understanding about what they do and what their priorities should be, away from pastoring as management toward pastoring as "cure of souls."

Peterson notes that the primary sense of *cura* in Latin is "care," with undertones of "cure." He writes, "The soul is the essence of the human personality. The cure of souls, then, is the Scripture-directed, prayer-shaped care that is devoted to persons singly or in groups, in settings sacred and profane."[7] He argues that cure of souls

> is not a narrowing of pastoral work to its devotional aspects, but it is a way of life that uses weekday tasks, encounters, and situations as the raw material for teaching prayer, developing faith, and preparing for a good death. . . . It is also a term that identifies us with our ancestors and colleagues in ministry, lay and clerical, who are convinced that a life of prayer is the connective tissue between holy day proclamation and weekday discipleship.[8]

According to Peterson, "weekday tasks, encounters, and situations" are the fuel for teaching faith and discipleship, and prayer is the "connective tissue" between Sunday worship and weekday life. He is talking about the intersection of everyday life and our life in God, just as Ammerman does, but using different language to express it.

My earliest experiences offering pastoral care came in the first years after I graduated from college, when I served with a ministry to college students. In those years, praying with a student after a pastoral care conversation always meant intercessory prayer. The student might not feel comfortable praying out loud, but I prayed extemporaneously for the student and then gave the student the opportunity to pray if they felt comfortable.

Later, as a minister, I often used that same pattern of extemporaneous intercessory prayer. In addition, I experimented with leading people into other forms of prayer. One of my favorites is breath prayer, perhaps breathing out concerns into God's presence with each breath, and then imagining breathing in God's love and peace.

If prayer is the "connective tissue" between our daily life and Sunday worship, then a variety of forms of prayer are worth exploring in pastoral care settings. Peterson's metaphor of connective tissue evokes the body, and engaging the body in forms of prayer can be helpful in pastoral care settings. Breath prayer, of course, connects praying people with their body through their breath.

Sometimes I ask people to place their hands palm-up on their knees and imagine offering their concerns to God. Other times I ask people who are experiencing guilt or shame to write some notes about what they are experiencing, and then we burn the paper in a bowl, asking God to take away those feelings.

In addition to describing prayer as connective tissue, Peterson suggests adopting both an attitude and a series of questions that he believes should guide pastoral work. Cure of souls, he writes,

 is a cultivated awareness that God has already seized the initiative. . . . Cure-of-souls questions are: What has God been doing here? What traces of grace can I discern in this life? What history of love can I read in this group? What has God set in motion that I can get in on?[9]

If God is already at work in every setting and situation, then helping *Crucial* people see the overlap between their daily life and God's presence is an exciting, hopeful task.

Pastoral care is sometimes viewed as helping people solve their problems, whether practical, emotional, or spiritual. Pastoral care might then focus on delivering a meal, sitting in an office at church offering care based in psychotherapeutic models, or steering someone to an appropriate Bible passage. All of those are good things in themselves.

Peterson adds an additional perspective when he encourages us to stop and look for God's grace and action already present in the situation. Paying attention to what God has already set in motion

Because of Eugene Peterson's influence, I developed a series of questions I often ask in pastoral care settings:

- In what ways do you pray about the situation you've just described?
- Are there other ways you could pray about it?
- Could we brainstorm some of those new ways?

Then I suggest that we pray at some length about the situation, using old and new ideas for prayer.

shifts the perspective of the carer from a problem-centered approach to curious, attentive, and mindful expectation that because of the miracle of God's incarnation in Jesus Christ, God is with us here and now.

Hope and Pastoral Care

I've told you about two authors who shaped my perspective on pastoral care. Nancy Ammerman helped me understand the significance of conversations that give people the opportunity to perceive and explore the overlaps or intersections of God and daily life. Eugene Peterson stresses a life of prayer as the connective tissue between Sunday worship and daily discipleship, and he advocates an understanding of pastoral care as cure of souls.

These themes, and many others discussed in this volume, are building blocks of hope. I want to tell you about my sixteen-year battle with depression and the ways I experienced hope through many different forms of pastoral care. This story illustrates the way pastoral care brings hope, sometimes without solving the presenting problem. My story also gives you the chance to get to know me a little. I will be your guide through the presentation of many issues related to pastoral care today, and knowing some of my background will help you to see the way my words come from my own life.

I was twenty-seven when I became pregnant with my first son. At about the four-month mark in the pregnancy, I started crying for long periods of time, particularly in the middle of the night. I had no idea what I was experiencing. I thought perhaps this was normal during pregnancy.

After our son's birth, I felt better for some months, then became discouraged and despondent again, which continued through my second pregnancy. After my second son was born, I again felt better for some months, but the dark feelings came back as he entered toddlerhood. For many years, I didn't know what to call this black cloud that came and went. I now know it was depression.

After sixteen years, my depression ended when I figured out that I have a B-vitamin deficiency, an unusual cause of depression. Evidently in my first pregnancy, my body gave my fragile B-vitamin stores to the baby—which I'm grateful for—leaving me deficient. For the past two decades I have taken B vitamins every day, and in those years I have experienced depression only a handful of times, for short periods, always triggered by extreme stress.

One characteristic of depression is lack of hope, and when I think back on my years of depression, I can attest to the profound absence of hope and the presence of feelings of despair and loss. One of the rays of hope, about five years into my depression, came from an inner-healing ministry I participated in.

Two women at a church I had formerly attended led a weekly group focused on inner-healing prayer, and I learned a great deal about God as healer. I had significant moments in that group when I felt God healing me from past hurts. I didn't recover from the depression, but I had a new sense of God's companionship, encouragement, and desire for good things in my life.

> A life of prayer is the connective tissue between holy day proclamation and weekday discipleship.
>
> —Eugene Peterson, "Curing Souls: The Forgotten Art" [10]

Another ray of hope came from an eating-disorders group I participated in for eighteen months about a decade into my depression. I learned about the group at a conference on spiritual growth held at Seattle Pacific University. At the conference, I attended a seminar on Christians and eating disorders. The seminar helped me understand that the overeating I engaged in as a way to cope with feeling bad about life was actually a form of eating disorder. The speaker told us about a group she led, and I joined it.

In the group we supported each other, and I learned a great deal about how eating disorders work. Again, my depression didn't go away, but I had hope that there were solutions for my cycle of feeling bad, eating too much to cope with the negative feelings, and then feeling bad again because I had overeaten.

The brightest rays of hope during my depression came from the small groups I participated in. For most of those years, I was in a support group for young moms in my congregation, and for about half of those years, my husband and I were also in a couple's small group.

The people in those groups deserve a big gold star for the countless times they listened to me talk about struggles in my life, for the many times they prayed for me, and for the words of encouragement and support they gave me. They gave me space, over and over, to talk honestly about my confusion about what God was doing in my life. They prayed for me in ways that felt deeply moving. I don't know how I could have survived those dark years without the support, week in and week out, from those wonderful people.

In my dark years, bits of hope came from other places as well, especially from a minister who entrusted me with leadership roles and trust, and a director of pastoral care who often encouraged me by describing things about me that she appreciated.

Gaining confidence in God's desire to heal, which I experienced in the inner-healing group, brought me hope and helped me learn new prayer patterns and new ways to see God's presence in the painful parts of my daily life. Hope also came from gaining information about the things that I was struggling with, which I experienced in the eating-disorders group. In addition, having prayer support, encouragement, and a listening ear in my small groups and elsewhere brought me hope.

My story illustrates many of the components of pastoral care that bring hope in the midst of pain. The forms of support I experienced from a wide variety of people include prayer, information, listening, trust, and encouragement. All of these helped me see new and hopeful things about the overlap between my daily life and God's presence with me. The care I received helped me continue to pray, even in the darkness, and helped me to see God's presence in my life and to continue to expect God to work in my life.

My depression didn't go away until I figured out the physiological key, my B-vitamin deficiency, so someone with an agenda to heal me would have been frustrated. However, someone with an agenda of bringing hope through pastoral care would have had ample opportunities to help me. I am deeply grateful for all the people who provided care to me in those years, and those people are in my mind as I write this book.

Looking Ahead

Nurturing Hope: Christian Pastoral Care in the Twenty-First Century is the first in a series of helpful and timely books, each of which addresses specific pastoral care needs in our complex and rapidly changing world. The series is called Living with Hope, and all of the books in the series are grounded in an understanding of pastoral care as a hopeful and encouraging endeavor, both for the carers and the care recipients.

This volume is divided into two parts. Part 1 presents seven changes in pastoral care patterns in recent years and their impact on pastoral care today, using many stories of individuals and groups who are doing pastoral care well. I have touched on those changes in this introductory chapter.

May the God of hope fill you with all joy and peace in believing, so that you may abound in hope by the power of the Holy Spirit.

—Romans 15:13

The seven changes in pastoral care patterns include shifts in who delivers pastoral care, the attitudes and commitments that undergird pastoral care, and some societal trends that are shaping pastoral care today. The practice of pastoral care has changed a great deal in recent years, and those changes need to be front and center for pastoral carers today. Understanding the changes helps alleviate some of the frustrations of pastoral care and also illuminates the significance of the pastoral care skills necessary for healthy and effective pastoral care in our time.

Part 2 presents four central pastoral care skills that are accessible for all. The work of Nancy Ammerman and Eugene Peterson provides an excellent platform for the four major pastoral care skills that make up the second half of this book with their focus on the connections between everyday life and Christian faith. The skills in part 2 help carers create and nurture those connections.

Understanding common stressors is the first key skill discussed in part 2. When people experience stress, God often feels distant, and the faith-based coping skills they are used to using seem to stop working. God and daily life seem disconnected. Prayer can feel difficult. One aspect of pastoral care is to help people find their way back to God in the midst of the stress. Therefore, the carer needs to understand sources of stress today and the emotional, spiritual, and physical effects of that stress.

A second major skill for pastoral carers is listening. How do we draw people out appropriately, so they can talk about God's presence in daily life? What does effective listening in pastoral care settings look like? Listening in pastoral care includes specific skills, such as reflecting back what we're hearing and asking gently probing questions. Another central listening skill for pastoral care involves learning to set aside the inner noise that crowds our minds when we hear other people's stories. We also need to use listening skills wisely so we, the carers, don't take ownership of other people's problems.

A third major skill explored in this book relates to spiritual practices. Carers need to feel comfortable praying with others in a variety of ways. Carers also need to be able to discuss the role of spiritual practices in daily life and help people find practices that work for them. After all, for many people, their spiritual practices are the times and places when they most consistently experience God's presence in daily life. If prayer is the connective tissue between Sunday worship and daily life, or between God and daily life, then we need to nourish that connection.

The carer's own spiritual practices also matter a great deal in pastoral care. If pastoral care involves paying attention to where God is already present, we need to nurture the habits and practices that make it more likely we will perceive God's presence. If our care is going to be grounded in the grace of the Triune God, then we need to be continually growing in our own patterns of drawing near to our loving God.

A final significant skill for pastoral caregivers relates to habits and rhythms that nurture resilience. Pastoral carers need support structures and patterns of rest and re-creation, so they can continue to care and give. They also need to know when the situation they are hearing about is too complex for their knowledge and skills, so referral is necessary.

I pray that this exploration of trends and skills presented will give you enthusiasm for the opportunities and gifts of being both a pastoral caregiver and pastoral care recipient in our time. I pray that

Training Tips

If you lead training sessions for pastoral carers, be sure to

1 Give them time to explore and discuss various purposes of pastoral care.

2 Give them a chance to brainstorm settings in your congregation where conversations about the overlap of daily life and the holy take place, and the kinds of questions that help to make those conversations happen.

3 Help them explore ways to become more comfortable praying with care recipients.

this exploration of pastoral care will bring you hope for your caring role and for your own spiritual journey.

For Reflection and Discussion

1 What have you observed about shifts in pastoral care in recent years? How do those shifts impact your ministry, your involvement in small groups, or your caring relationships in other settings?

2 How would you answer the question, "What is the purpose of pastoral care?"

3 With whom have you talked about the intersection between your daily life and your sense of the holy or sacred? In what settings did those conversations happen? What circumstances, questions, and forms of listening fostered the conversations?

4 What do you love about pastoral care? What do you find most difficult? Write out a prayer for yourself as a pastoral carer.

Resources

Dykstra, Robert C., ed. *Images of Pastoral Care*. St. Louis, MO: Chalice, 2005.

> Each of the nineteen contributors focuses on a metaphor for carers, including the solicitous shepherd, the wounded healer, the intimate stranger, and the midwife.

Cooper-White, Pamela. *Shared Wisdom: Use of the Self in Pastoral Care and Counseling*. Minneapolis: Fortress Press, 2004.

> Uses insights from new areas of study, including intersubjectivity and multicultural dynamics, to explore the ways a carer's personal issues and emotional reactions impact pastoral care.

Part One

Shifts in Pastoral Care in the Twenty-First Century

1

Pastoral Care Has Many Models

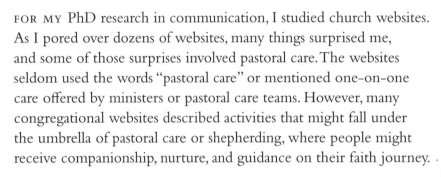

FOR MY PhD research in communication, I studied church websites. As I pored over dozens of websites, many things surprised me, and some of those surprises involved pastoral care. The websites seldom used the words "pastoral care" or mentioned one-on-one care offered by ministers or pastoral care teams. However, many congregational websites described activities that might fall under the umbrella of pastoral care or shepherding, where people might receive companionship, nurture, and guidance on their faith journey.

Several congregations I studied hosted support groups for adoptive parents, and one of them had three separate groups for parents who had adopted within the United States, from Asia, and from other countries around the world. I had never considered that the location of adoption would make a difference in the challenges for the adoptive parents, but with a few moments of reflection, I could imagine some of the issues parents might be dealing with. I was impressed by this level of care.

One congregation offered a support group for infertile couples. Several offered support groups for people who were grieving, and one congregation had a seminar in December about grief during the holidays. Several congregations offered classes in managing money and debt. I saw announcements on church websites for seminars on thriving with teenagers, helping aging parents, coping with chronic illness, and how to write a spiritual autobiography. Marriage enrichment opportunities included classes and seminars

21

on marriage, marriage mentoring programs, the Marriage Course sponsored by Alpha,[1] and various programs for engaged couples.

It was clear from the church websites that people from both within and outside the congregation would be welcome. The boundaries around congregations are increasingly porous, as more people attend church intermittently and as more families of churchgoers include people with different religious commitments who might come along with relatives to a church activity that interests them.

Many people hold a model of pastoral care involving an ordained minister visiting a parishioner in their home or having a conversation with a church member in the church office. That model stands in contrast with the patterns I observed on church websites—congregations' porous boundaries, multiple and varied opportunities for learning and connection with others, and the many lay people who lead classes and groups.

Definitions of Pastoral Care

If pastoral care is understood so broadly that it includes support groups for adoptive parents and recommendations from ministers for books on mindfulness meditation, what exactly is pastoral care? I argued in the introduction that Christian pastoral care today must include a faith-based perspective that sees pastoral care as soul care and that makes space for people to talk about God's presence in daily life. Many writers argue that most Christians have an intuitive sense of what pastoral care is, but they say defining it precisely is quite difficult.

A landmark book, *Pastoral Care in Historical Perspective*, published in 1964, has been revised many times and is still in print and widely read. It was the first book to systematically analyze pastoral care over nineteen centuries of Christian history. The authors, William Clebsch and Charles Jaekle, propose a definition for pastoral care that has influenced at least two generations of ministers and pastoral carers: "Pastoral Care consists of helping acts, done by representative

Bear one another's burdens, and in this way you will fulfill the law of Christ.

—Galatians 6:2

disconcerting

Christian persons, directed toward the healing, sustaining, guiding and reconciling of (troubled persons) whose troubles arise in the context of ultimate meanings and concerns."[2]

When I taught students about pastoral care, they latched on to the four verbs in the definition: healing, sustaining, guiding, and reconciling. In class discussion and essays, my students enthusiastically described and analyzed various forms of pastoral care ministry in the light of those verbs. Emmanuel Lartey, a seminary professor who writes about intercultural approaches to pastoral care, notes that another writer adds a fifth verb, nurturing. Lartey proposes adding two more verbs: liberating and empowering.[3]

Because the Clebsch and Jaekle definition, with the possible addition of three more verbs, has influenced so many pastoral carers, the components of the definition are worth pondering in the light of shifts in pastoral care in the past few decades.

Stephen Pattison, a British pastoral theologian who has written widely about pastoral care, presents and discusses critiques of Clebsch and Jaekle's definition.[4] I draw on Pattison's critiques below as I walk through the components of the definition. Many of these critiques I describe relate to the trends in pastoral care that are explored in the first half of this book.

First, note that the two authors view pastoral care as help "done (1) by representative Christian persons." When I was ordained as a Presbyterian minister in 1997, my view of pastoral care was strongly influenced by this perspective. I considered pastoral care to be actions done by a minister or the lay pastoral care team at the church where I worked. The lay carers on the team represented the congregation in some capacity, thus conveying to care recipients that the care was coming from the congregation in some semiofficial way.

I was surprised the first time I heard someone say, "Most pastoral care today happens in small groups"—the kinds of groups I later saw

Be hospitable to one another.

—1 Peter 4:9

mentioned when I explored church websites. It took me quite a few ✓ years to wrap my mind around the clear truth that in congregations, small groups are the setting for a lot of healing, sustaining, guiding, reconciling, nurturing, liberating, and empowering.

Small-group members would not view themselves as "representative persons" of their congregation, and they would probably not use the words "pastoral care" for the way they support each other, yet they provide so much care, as do congregation members in many other settings when they engage in a nurturing way with each other. Therefore, the notion of pastoral care being delivered only or *exactly* mostly by "representative persons" is no longer accurate. ①

Misconceptions:

> Much of the task of pastoral care is to help people see where God is already at work and how they can join in.

Second, looking again at the Clebsch and Jaekle definition, consider the use of the words "troubled persons" ② to describe pastoral care recipients. What about the person who wants to pray more deeply or love a spouse more consistently? Must that person be viewed as "troubled" in order to receive pastoral care?

Eugene Peterson believes that we limit pastoral ministry when we focus it only on people who we perceive to be troubled. Rather, *great* much of the task of pastoral care is to help people see where God is ② already at work and how they can join in.

Peterson recommends that pastoral carers ask "cure of soul" questions like: "What has God been doing here? What traces of grace can I discern in this life? What history of love can I read in this group? What has God set in motion that I can get in on?"[5] These questions show that sometimes pastoral carers have the great *Yes!.* privilege of nurturing people in situations where good things are already happening.

Third, look at the closing phrase of the definition: "whose ③ troubles arise in the context of ultimate meanings and concerns." Personally, I like nothing better than talking with people about ultimate meanings and concerns, and Christian pastoral care often includes deep conversations that may help people trust and pray to the God in whom we find ultimate meaning. But what about someone

Helping a person with dinner or a utility bill is not excluded from pastoral care just because the troubles did not arise in an area of ultimate significance.

who can't pay a utility bill because of an unexpected job layoff? What about someone who is just home from the hospital and can't cook dinner? Helping a person with dinner or a utility bill is not excluded from pastoral care just because the troubles did not arise in an area of ultimate significance.

A fourth concern about the Clebsch and Jaekle definition relates to the individualism implicit in the definition. Much pastoral care does involve helping individuals, but often pastoral care also involves families, extended families, neighborhoods, and communities. Sometimes pastoral care involves considering social-justice issues that are rooted in situations involving many people.

In response to the Clebsch and Jaekle definition of pastoral care, Pattison proposes his own definition, saying that "pastoral care is that activity, undertaken especially by representative persons, directed toward the elimination and relief of sin and sorrow and the presentation of all people perfect in Christ to God."[6]

His phrase "elimination and relief of sin and sorrow" relates to the pain and struggles so many pastoral care recipients experience, and can include both individuals and groups of people. His words "the presentation of all people perfect in Christ to God" refer to all the ways pastoral care can help people grow in faith, whether or not they consider themselves to be troubled or in need.

Pattison's definition retains the special role of "representative persons"—ministers and pastoral care teams trained and sent out by congregations—while acknowledging that other people are often involved in pastoral care.

Because definitions can help pastoral carers understand the task they have undertaken, even simpler definitions may be more useful, and certainly easier to remember. I found a descriptive statement about pastoral care, not intended as a definition, that actually works fairly well to help pastoral carers understand what they are doing. Seminary professor Barbara McClure notes that "pastoral care has *better* historically included any activity of the church that meets the needs of its members and its community."[8]

The Rise of Pastoral Counseling

Inspired by the many "one another" passages in the New Testament, Christians have always taken seriously the call to meet the needs inside and outside the Christian community, to be kind and compassionate to one another (Eph 4:32), to bear one another's burdens (Gal 6:2), and to offer hospitality to one another (1 Pet 4:9). Throughout the ages, lay people have taken these commands seriously and tried to care for and support each other. In addition, priests, ministers, monks, and nuns have always had a special role in providing care through visitation, practical help, and spiritual guidance.

While numerous theologians have written with diverse points of view about pastoral care over the first 1,900 years of church history, most writers acknowledge that something significant changed in the middle of the twentieth century. At that time, pastoral care came to ← *mid-20th c* be understood as primarily the responsibility of ordained ministers as they offered pastoral counseling to individuals.

Pastoral counseling, as practiced in the twentieth century, involves applying insights from psychology to the work of the clergy. Seward Hiltner was a key figure in advocating this perspective. He wrote ten books and five hundred articles describing and promoting pastoral counseling. When he died in 1984 at the age of seventy-four, his influence was so strong that he had an obituary in the *New York Times*.[9]

In 1949, Hiltner defined pastoral counseling in a way that has influenced many ministers: "The attempt by a pastor to help people help themselves through the process of gaining an understanding of inner conflicts."[10] The critiques of his definition that arose in the later decades of the twentieth century and the early twenty-first century include many of the issues that will be explored in this book.

> Blessed be the God and Father of our Lord Jesus Christ, the Father of mercies and the God of all consolation, who consoles us in all our affliction, so that we may be able to console those who are in any affliction with the consolation with which we ourselves are consoled by God.
>
> —2 Corinthians 1:3–4

critique

Like the definition of pastoral care from Clebsch and Jaekle, Hiltner's description of pastoral counseling is individualistic and minister-centric. In addition, his definition focuses only on resolving inner conflicts. God and the Christian faith journey—or even the "ultimate meanings and concerns" that Clebsch and Jaekle mention—are completely lacking in the definition.

Bonnie J. Miller-McLemore, in a *Christian Century* article where she reflects on her transition from being a graduate student to seminary teacher, describes this shift to pastoral counseling in the middle of the twentieth century:

> Whereas in 1939 few theological schools offered counseling courses, by the 1950s almost all of them did. And 80 percent listed additional courses in psychology and had at least one psychologist on staff. For a brief period in the 1960s and 1970s, Carl Roger's *Counseling and Psychotherapy* was a standard text.[11]

She points out that in the 1970s and 1980s, the most common replacement for Rogers's book was Howard Clinebell's *Basic Types of Pastoral Care and Counseling.* In it, "most of the text is devoted to particular counseling techniques for an array of problems."[12]

In the twenty-first century, writers and practitioners in the area of pastoral care see Christian pastoral care much more broadly, communally, and holistically, with an emphasis on faith in the Triune God, who is present with us in all ministry. Pastoral counseling, as defined by Hiltner, is only one of many forms of pastoral care today.

Overlaps with Other Ministries

The communal and holistic nature of pastoral care today is visible in the kinds of relationships nurtured by the marriage enrichment courses and support groups for adoptive parents that I found on church websites. Seminars on coping with aging parents or chronic illnesses also provide a vivid contrast to the view of pastoral care primarily as a minister and an individual sitting in a church office talking about inner conflicts.

> Pastoral care is, in essence, surprisingly simple. It has one fundamental aim: to help people know love, both something to be received and something to give.
>
> —Alastair V. Campbell, *Professionalism and Pastoral Care*[7]

Important as this twentieth-century focus on pastoral counseling as a ministry to troubled persons has been, it has unfortunately meant at times a concomitant lack of focus on nurturing the development of more ordinary, relatively healthy people. Pastoral care needs to have as its primary focus the care of all God's people through the ups and downs of everyday life, the engendering of caring environments within which all people can grow and develop to their fullest potential. Not all of God's people need pastoral *counsel*; all people, however, need the nurture and support of a *caring* environment.

—Charles Gerkin, *An Introduction to Pastoral Care*[13]

I know of several congregations that have devoted space on their property to gardens where people in the community can grow vegetables and flowers. Residents of the local community and congregation members get to know one another as they work together in the garden. Conversations develop over time, and congregation members become aware of various physical, practical, emotional, and spiritual needs among people who do not attend the congregation. Often, congregational members and leaders help meet those needs or steer people toward resources where those needs can be met.

Are community gardens—and the relationships that form as church members and residents of the neighborhood work together—local mission or pastoral care? The answer must be both. In much of the twentieth century, pastoral care was viewed as something that happens within a congregation, and mission was perceived as an activity that takes place outside the congregation, and in fact mostly overseas. Gradually congregational leaders began to understand that many places in local cities and towns are in need of help, so their mission field begins right outside their door.

At the same time as congregations have come to understand that mission work is needed close at hand, pastoral care in our secular age has moved beyond the congregation. Connections have been made between congregations and local schools, youth centers, prisons, neighborhood and city advocacy groups, and other community institutions and organizations, and relationships have formed, allowing for caring interactions that fit the pattern of pastoral care. As these overlaps have occurred, pastoral care and mission have joined hands. In the chapters that follow, I will present many more examples of pastoral care outside congregations.

Newcomer programs in congregations provide another illustration of the way that boundaries between pastoral care and other ministries have become more porous. In the introductory chapter, I mentioned Leah, the director of congregational care at a church that has a formal program for new members. Leah oversees six hours of instruction for prospective new members, which takes place either in four sessions on consecutive Sunday mornings or as a Friday evening and Saturday morning event.

This class is required for all new members, and people who are considering membership often attend. The purpose of the class is threefold, to help new members and prospective members

- learn how the congregation works and what ministries are offered;
- think about their own spiritual gifts and how they might get involved in the congregation's ministries and mission; and
- help group members get to know each other.

Because of the relational style that Leah uses as she leads the class, each class of new members generally bonds. Leah has found that some friendships created in the class last for many years.

Is this class a ministry to new members or is it pastoral care? Again, the answer must be "both." A similar question could be asked about many music ministries where the musicians gather before rehearsal to share briefly and pray together, or when they stick around after the rehearsal to catch up on each other's lives. Is that music ministry or pastoral care? Both.

With good leadership, and with an understanding by congregational members of their call to care for each other, almost any

Often pastoral care also involves families, extended families, neighborhoods, and communities.

congregational activity can have pastoral care components if we
analyze those activities using the verbs healing, sustaining, guiding,
reconciling, nurturing, liberating, and empowering. Or, to go
back to the research of Nancy Tatom Ammerman described in
the introduction, settings for pastoral care include all places where
people can talk about the overlap of their faith and their daily life,
and those settings abound.

active

Pastoral Care as Lament

To illustrate another aspect of pastoral care in our time, I'll mention
a friend of mine who has taught pastoral care in several settings. The
first reading she assigns to her students is a brief magazine article by
Henri Nouwen, Roman Catholic priest and prolific writer, entitled
"Care." Nouwen writes about the deep need most of us feel to offer
advice, solutions, or cures when we encounter someone in pain.
He also describes the strong urge most of us have to run away from
painful realities, particularly if we are unable to change them.

Nouwen then describes a different pattern:

> The friend who can be silent with us in a moment of despair
> or confusion, who can stay with us in an hour of grief and
> bereavement, who can tolerate not-knowing, not-curing, not-
> healing and face with us the reality of our powerlessness, that is the
> friend who cares.[14]

Locate article

Nouwen argues that caring involves allowing the other person to
come close to us, to enter into communion with us, to share pain
without our necessarily fixing it. This journeying together changes
the power dynamic within a caring relationship, because "we tend
to look at caring as an attitude of the strong to the weak, of the
powerful toward the powerless, of the have's to the have-not's. And,
in fact, we feel quite uncomfortable with an invitation to enter into
someone's pain before doing something about it."[15]

Pastoral care in our time has been shaped by a growing
understanding of the negative repercussions of unequal power

Impt topic — find resources

Many small groups in congregations—Bible study groups, prayer groups, book groups, and various task groups—are places where people give and receive pastoral care. They grieve with each other. They cry out together. They share each other's journeys.

relationships, a trend that will be discussed in chapter 6. You can see why my friend opens her courses on pastoral care with Nouwen's perspective. In addition to his mention of power relationships, he challenges the expectation that pastoral care always involves helping or curing. He illuminates the fact that anyone who comes near to someone in need, who is willing to grieve with them, is giving care. That kind of care can happen in many different settings.

The many classes, seminars, and support groups I mentioned at the beginning of this chapter provide settings for people to connect with each other on a shared journey. Nouwen believes that <u>the basic meaning of the word "care" is to lament with another person</u>, "to grieve, to experience sorrow, to cry out with."[16] Many small groups in congregations—Bible study groups, prayer groups, book groups, and various task groups—are places where people give and receive pastoral care. They grieve with each other. They cry out together. They share each other's journeys.

Pastoral care is no longer the sole province of ordained clergy, and in the next chapter I will develop this idea further as I explore the role of lay people and lay teams in pastoral care. Christian pastoral care today happens in many settings inside and outside congregations. Pastoral care can involve solving problems and helping people face inner conflicts. In addition, it includes many

---

Training Tips

If you lead training sessions for pastoral carers,

1 Discuss possible definitions of the seven verbs associated with pastoral care: healing, sustaining, guiding, reconciling, nurturing, liberating, and empowering. Discuss what they look like in practice.

2 Look over the various definitions of pastoral care presented in this chapter. Help participants identify the characteristics of the definitions that enable them to understand the task of pastoral care today.

3 Help pastoral carers explore the emotions they feel when powerless, when they are "not-knowing, not-curing, not-healing," and how to set those emotions aside to be present with care recipients.

kinds of mutual support and encouragement for spiritual growth. Pastoral care can involve simply mourning with others.

For Reflection and Discussion

1 What creative or unexpected forms of Christian pastoral care have you observed? In what ways do you think they work well or do not work well?

2 Are you comfortable receiving care as well as giving it? What obstacles make it difficult for you to receive care? What has helped you learn to receive care? What might help?

3 Does the pastoral counseling model impact your own practice of pastoral care? If so, what are the benefits and hindrances that model creates for you?

4 How do you respond to the idea that one aspect of pastoral care is to lament with others, without trying to fix them? What challenges do you experience when you are faced with "not-knowing, not-curing, not-healing" and become aware of your powerlessness? Write a prayer for yourself as a pastoral carer who laments with others.

Resources

Gerkin, Charles. *An Introduction to Pastoral Care*. Nashville: Abingdon, 1997.

> An introduction to the history, theory, and practice of pastoral care. Gerkin argues that care is "the central metaphor of life in the Christian community."

Hunter, Rodney J. *Dictionary of Pastoral Care and Counseling*. 3rd ed. Nashville: Abingdon, 1990.

> A reference book with more than 1,200 theoretical and practical entries about pastoral care and counseling.

2

Teams and a Variety of Individuals Provide Pastoral Care

TWENTY YEARS ago, my husband, Dave, was nominated for and then elected to the Board of Deacons in the Presbyterian congregation in Seattle where I was an associate pastor. Congregations in the Presbyterian Church (USA) have both elders and deacons who serve on two very different boards. The elders are charged with leadership and governance, and the deacons are charged with service.

The form of service the deacons choose to embrace varies greatly from one congregation to another. In the Presbyterian congregation we attended as young adults, the deacons focused on two tasks: sending birthday cards to church members and helping with food for funerals. In the congregation where my husband was elected a deacon, the Board of Deacons functioned as a lay pastoral care team with a variety of responsibilities.

Dave is one of the kindest-hearted people on the face of the earth, with gifts of service and compassion. A decade earlier, he had served for one three-year term as an elder. The governance and leadership tasks of an elder, along with some conflict that occurred during his term, drained him so profoundly that when the time came to commit to a second term, he said no.

He knew that being a deacon would be different, but he still had reservations. Within a few months, he was euphoric. Here, at last, was a church ministry that dovetailed with his gifts, desires, and

Pastoral care is not performed only by the pastor. It is a task also for the laity. Taking seriously Luther's belief in the priesthood of all believers, pastoral care empowers the laity to strengthen the caring done by a congregation.

—Howard Stone, *Theological Context for Pastoral Caregiving: Word in Deed*[1]

concerns. Because of his enthusiasm, he and I often joked that he was the poster boy for deacons.

A Pastoral Care Team

The deacons in our congregation delivered a lot of meals to people who were ill or housebound, or who had just had babies. They had been doing this for years, and they had a well-developed system. Every quarter, they met on a Saturday morning for a "cook-off," where they prepared soup, stew, and casseroles, which they froze in various portion sizes. Clear and easily accessible records were kept.

Whenever someone in the congregation needed a meal, the meal coordinator contacted one or two deacons to deliver a meal. Deacons would stop by the church, extract a main dish or two from the freezer, make a note in the records, purchase some salad and bread, then deliver the meal. If possible and if appropriate, when they delivered the meal, the deacons would visit with the person or family and pray with them.

Deacons also served communion in Sunday worship services, and after communion services, several deacons delivered communion to shut-ins and people who were ill. The deacons sometimes helped with practical tasks like helping someone move or driving someone to a medical appointment. The board of deacons received oversight from a church staff member, the director of pastoral care, who trained new deacons to take communion into homes and to talk and pray with people in need.

The director of pastoral care attended the monthly Board of Deacons meeting, bringing current needs to the deacons and sometimes doing some training at the meetings. The congregation also had a Stephen Ministry program, and sometimes a Stephen minister conducted training about listening. Stephen Ministry is a program that creates a structure for congregation members to be trained in listening skills and then paired with someone who needs a listening ear.[2]

Dave loved the sense of teamwork with other deacons. He found the cook-offs fun because he was cooking along with others. He enjoyed the monthly meetings because so many of the other deacons had gifts and passions similar to his. Because of relationships with them, and because of the training by the director of pastoral care, he felt that he was growing in pastoral care skills. The monthly meetings always included an extended time of prayer for people in need in the congregation, and Dave appreciated that a team of people were entrusting people's needs into the hands of God.

He found it rewarding to take meals to people, chatting with them and praying with them. Serving communion in worship services, and sharing communion with people in their homes or in nursing homes, felt like some of the biggest privileges he had ever experienced. He called these occasions "holy ground."

When his three-year term ended, he happily renewed for a second term. And later, when we moved a new city, he looked around the congregation we joined for a similar task to engage in. The closest parallel involved signing up to make meals for people and deliver them.

For eighteen months, Dave prepared meals a couple of times a month for a family where the mother—exactly his own age—had Lou Gehrig's disease. In the early months of her disease, she was home alone all day, so he often stayed with her for an hour, listening to her concerns and praying with her. As her disease progressed and she could no longer talk, he still stayed to visit for a while when he dropped off a meal. He read the Bible to her and prayed for her. When she died, he felt that he had lost a friend.

I'm grateful that congregation had a system to bring meals to people in need. I had two major surgeries while we were in that congregation, and the meals people brought over helped me to feel loved and cared for.

Meals are vitally important, but Dave found that after his friend with Lou Gehrig's disease died, he lost heart for the meal ministry. It took him a while to figure out the reasons it felt unsatisfying to him.

In most instances, people were too busy to stop and talk when he delivered a meal. The ability to express care through listening and prayer had been the most fulfilling aspect of the whole process for Dave. He had no feeling of teamwork with others doing the same kind of service. He didn't even know the names of the other people on the meal-delivery list because they never met together. He missed praying together with other carers, committing people's needs to God. He also felt the lack of growth in pastoral care skills with others that training would have provided.

That congregation also had another interesting pastoral care initiative. For several years, the experienced gardeners in the congregation made themselves available in the spring to help people start vegetable gardens. Several of them would arrive on a Saturday, prepare the soil, plant the vegetables, and give some instructions to the family for how to care for the new garden. I always regretted that Dave had no interest or skills in gardening, because that form of pastoral care was team-based and more relational than delivering meals.

In Christian theology care goes with baptism and not ordination. A misplaced identification of care with the ordained has made care a matter of having a special gift of knowledge. . . . The point here is that ordinary care became neglected, if not disdained.

—Peggy Way, *Created by God: Pastoral Care for All God's People*[3]

Why Pastoral Care Teams Matter

Whenever I hear about a congregation without a pastoral care team, I feel sad. In most cases in those congregations, the minister is expected to do most or all of the pastoral care as part of a job description that in our era includes many other tasks as well.

Tim Farabaugh, a former seminary professor who currently directs a community for seniors, describes the relative simplicity of the pastoral task in years past. He writes that for most of church history, "the role of the pastor meant leading of worship and the visitation of the sick and dying. Pastors visited those in need and generally went from home to home to minister to those within the pastoral flock."[4]

He also describes the pressures that ministers face today that were unknown in years past:

> In other times, clergy lived with different time demands. For example, they did not face long commutes to hospitals or traffic jams. They did not have multilevel administrative meetings nor did they have to deal with local government zoning boards. Contemporary clergy need . . . a variety of continuing education courses not imagined fifty years ago. They need skills in planning and leadership and team building, fund development and community organization and sometimes, even plumbing skills. In many ways today, clergy are the least focused on the care of souls because of the many demands placed upon them.[5]

Because of the complexity of the task of leading congregations today, clergy need the help of lay people to build a healthy congregational community in many areas, not only pastoral care. Farabaugh provides a caveat for his words quoted above: "I am not saying that clergy today do not care for souls. . . . I am saying that today clergy and laity can work together in new and creative ways to care for souls. This is the team-based approach that we need."[6]

So impt

Howard Stone, a seminary professor who has written widely about pastoral care, notes that much of the literature about the role of ministers in pastoral care and counseling published in the four decades between 1950 and 1990 primarily treats the ministry of lay people within congregations "with superficiality and silence," ignoring the significance of the pastoral ministry of the whole congregation.[7] In the 1990s, though, the literature on the ministry of everyone within congregations began to blossom, addressing lay ministry in pastoral care as well as many other areas of congregational life.

We now understand that congregations are communities with a rich tapestry of varied gifts, as well as relationships and connections that are nurtured in diverse activities. People talk about the intersection between God and their daily life in many settings and with many different people, receiving and giving soul care in relationships that are often reciprocal. Many congregational activities provide settings for relationships with components of healing, sustaining, guiding, reconciling, nurturing, liberating, and empowering.

Ministers trained in seminaries between 1950 and 1990 must be forgiven if they have taken some time to grasp the significance of lay ministry teams in many areas of congregational life. In those four decades, almost two generations of clergy were shaped by an emphasis on pastoral counseling as the central task of pastoral care, along with "superficiality and silence" about the significance of the ministry of congregation members.

Many older members in congregations today were shaped by expectations, common in the middle decades of the twentieth century, that their minister would do the majority of the work of pastoral care. In many cases, the congregational culture has to change to make way for a more collaborative form of ministry in this and many other areas of congregational life.

Like good stewards of the manifold grace of God, serve one another with whatever gift each of you has received.

—1 Peter 4:10

Spiritual Gifts

Why am I sad when I hear about a congregation where the minister is expected to do most of the pastoral care? I grieve when I see ordained ministers experiencing debilitating pressure to do everything, risking burnout, and I also grieve when I see people in their congregations who are not using their spiritual gifts.

Farabaugh reflects, "Lay pastoral care is based on the idea that the church wastes the gifts of community when it does not encourage and empower laity to use their gifts."[8] I think of my husband's kind heart and gifts of compassion and service. Like many people with a tender heart, Dave is not the kind of person who pushes himself forward. He thrives when he has a structure for serving, teammates to serve and learn with, and a congregational climate where the gifts and service of all members are talked about. Serving on a pastoral care team in our Seattle church gave him what he needed to serve enthusiastically.

I have observed that spiritual gifts come in clusters that together shape how the gifts are shared. For example, my husband has gifts of service and compassion, while my mother has gifts of service and administration. Both my husband and my mother have served in numerous pastoral care roles in their congregations. Both have taken communion into homes and nursing homes. Both have sat with and prayed with congregation members who are ill and helped other members of their congregations with practical needs.

The New Testament contains three lists of spiritual gifts, in Romans 12, 1 Corinthians 12, and Ephesians 4. Some interpreters view these as three lists of the same kinds of gifts, and others view them as lists of three different kinds of gifts. I have found benefit in both perspectives, and I really don't know how the apostle Paul and the early church viewed these lists of gifts. I do know that spiritual gifts must be acknowledged in some way in congregational life so that people can be encouraged to serve in areas where they have innate strengths and passions.

However, their style of care is different. My husband, with his gift of compassion, is more likely to listen deeply for long periods of time. He comes into pastoral care settings gently and pays attention to what's already going on. My mother, with her gift of administration, is more likely to be the one who sets up the list of people who will deliver communion or meals. She comes into pastoral care situations briskly and with contagious energy and enthusiasm. Both styles are valuable, and both patterns of service are shaped by spiritual gifts.

In our time, with so many pressures on ordained ministers, congregational leaders provide strong support for their ministers in many ways. When teams of lay people can take over some of the forms of ministry for which the clergy person is not most gifted, the minister receives a gift, as do the lay people. Yes, every Christian can visit a sick person, and every Christian should at times do so. Christians with gifts of service and compassion should do it more often than those with other gifts such as leadership and teaching.

Two or three decades ago, when people who study and support congregations began to promote lay pastoral care teams, they presumed that an ordained minister would supervise and train the teams. This sort of clergy involvement is not necessary, though.

Because of the clergy shortage in Roman Catholic churches, they have long employed pastoral care coordinators who are lay people. Increasingly, Protestant churches are doing the same, and I know a number of pastoral care coordinators who are not ordained. Some of them have theological education or training in counseling skills. Some of them have risen up through the ranks in their congregations, first serving on a pastoral care team, then growing into a leadership role.

Gene Fowler, a Presbyterian minister with a PhD in pastoral ministry who has written widely about pastoral care as well as congregational life, notes that "ordained and lay care ministry in the church are deeply intertwined with other aspects of ministry as well as with the communal life of the congregation."[9] Pastoral care

I grieve when I see ordained ministers experiencing debilitating pressure to do everything, risking burnout, and I also grieve when I see people in their congregations who are not using their spiritual gifts.

ministry in our time is woven into the fabric of congregational life, as people in small groups, support groups, task groups, committees, and music groups provide care for each other in a variety of congregational settings.

This has profound implications because all members are encouraged to use their gifts. All members can be equipped to serve effectively. The shift I'm describing in this chapter is a great gift both to lay people and to ordained ministers.

Settings for Pastoral Care

Fowler poses an interesting question: What constitutes a pastoral ← care conversation?[10] Can a chat in a casual context be as much a part of pastoral care as a conversation when planning a funeral or a counseling session in a minister's office? Can an email or even a Facebook post be considered pastoral care in some cases? I would answer "yes" to these questions with enthusiasm.

When I was a minister in a congregation, people often asked if they could talk with me about a problem. We would make an appointment to meet in my office or in a coffee shop, and I would listen. We talked about how to pray about the issue, and we prayed together.

I seldom met with anyone a second time. Instead, I checked in with them about the issue by email, in a phone conversation, or in person at coffee hour or after church meetings. Occasionally, quite a bit

In *Wishful Thinking*, Frederick Buechner brings together two ideas—our neighbor's needs and our gifts—in a discussion that relates to spiritual gifts. He writes that God calls you to "the kind of work (a) that you need most to do, and (b) that the world most needs to have done. . . . The place God calls you to is the place where your deep gladness and world's deep hunger meet."[11]

later, we might meet again to talk in person. I offered follow-up care in a variety of ways. Recently, as I was describing this pattern to a friend with a lot of experience in pastoral care, she reflected that this pattern probably helped care recipients not to feel dependent on me.

One incident from my time as a pastor illustrates the significance of online communication in pastoral care. A leader in our congregation lost his mother. We prayed for him in staff meetings, and the senior pastor, the director of pastoral care, and the missions pastor all tried to have conversations with him about his mourning process. But he wasn't willing to talk.

I happened to drop him an email about a financial matter, and in the email I asked, "How are you doing as you mourn the loss of your mother?" He wrote back with an extended email expressing his grief. He and I emailed back and forth several times about his grief process. He is a very reserved man and obviously felt more comfortable writing about his feelings rather than talking about them.

I have seen significant pastoral care on Facebook, as friends express their concern and their willingness to pray for people. Obviously only a small portion of Facebook posts, emails, and other online

Training Tips

If you lead training sessions for pastoral carers,

1   Help them explore their spiritual gifts and how they use them in pastoral care.

2   Discuss goals for teamwork in pastoral care, drawing out the hopes and expectations of trainees, and discussing what they can expect in the way of teamwork in the congregation. Help them think about ways they will contribute to the health of the pastoral care team.

3   Discuss the role of prayer on pastoral care teams, and explore the kinds of prayer members of your pastoral care team would appreciate.

conversations can be considered pastoral care, but some of them are. Some of them express the intersection of faith and daily life or allow others to express that connection.

Some online communications help people pray about their situations. Some have components of healing, sustaining, guiding, reconciling, nurturing, liberating, and empowering. They represent the web of relationships inside and outside congregations and the many connections people have with each other. This is a part of Christian pastoral care today, as pastoral care conversations happen in a variety of settings inside and outside congregations.

For Reflection and Discussion

1 What pastoral care teams or other ministry teams have you served on? What were the blessings and challenges of serving on a team?

2 How would you describe your own spiritual gifts? In what settings do you use them? How do your various gifts work together to shape your patterns of service?

3 Have you observed the presence or absence of congregational structures that work well to help people use their gifts? Aspects of congregational culture that discourage or encourage people to use their gifts? Describe the impact of these patterns.

4 Think of the kinds of settings where you have engaged in pastoral care conversations. Are there other settings you would like to explore? Write a prayer for yourself as a pastoral carer who is open to teamwork and willing to offer care in diverse settings.

Resources

Wimberly, John W., Jr. *Mobilizing Congregations: How Teams Can Motivate Members and Get Things Done.* Lanham, MD: Rowman & Littlefield, 2015.

A thorough and practical exploration of the ways teams help congregations, based in case studies. Wimberly is a consultant with the Congregational Consulting Group, and the book draws on his varied experience with congregations.

Weems, Lovett H., Jr. *Church Leadership: Vision, Team, Culture, Integrity.* Nashville: Abingdon, 2010.

Weems discusses recent research on organizational systems in the light of Christian theology and congregational culture. As he points out, congregational leaders have a significant impact on the teams within congregations.

Hartwig, Ryan T., and Warren Bird. *Teams That Thrive: Five Disciplines of Collaborative Church Leadership.* Downers Grove, IL: InterVarsity, 2015.

The authors present the characteristics of leadership teams in congregations of various sizes where team ministries thrive. They discuss structures and paradigms that undergird effective teams.

3

Christian Pastoral Care Is Grounded in the Triune God

GOD THE Shepherd is a vivid, encouraging metaphor for many people. Someone told me about a graveside service in the late 1980s, at the height of the AIDS epidemic, when most congregations did not welcome gay people. After the minister concluded the service for a gay man who had died of AIDS, one of the man's friends approached the minister and said, "There's something in your Bible about a shepherd. I remember it from when I was a kid. Could you please read it to me?"

The minister opened his Bible and read Psalm 23. The man stood beside the open grave with tears pouring down his face.

Because the word "pastoral" comes from a Latin word meaning "related to herdsmen or shepherds," I'll begin this chapter with a look at the way shepherding in the Bible informs our practice of Christian pastoral care today.

Shepherds in the Bible

Most Christians know the powerful shepherd metaphors from Psalm 23 and the passage in the Gospel of John where Jesus calls himself the Good Shepherd (John 10:1–18). The Bible contains 112 additional references to shepherds, and most of those, of course, refer simply to people who tend sheep. A surprising number, however, use the concept of shepherd as a metaphor. Ten passages refer to God as Shepherd, including the words from Psalm 80:1, "Give ear,

O Shepherd of Israel," and Isaiah 40:11, "He will feed his flock like a shepherd."

More than thirty times, *shepherd* in the Bible refers to leaders, often negatively, making a comparison between bad leaders and bad shepherds. For example, Matthew 9:36 describes Jesus's compassion for the crowds because they were like "sheep without a shepherd," a reference to several passages in the Hebrew Scriptures that use the same words (see Num 27:17, 1 Kgs 22:17, 2 Chr 18:16). Generations of Christian pastors have drawn on Jesus's words as they pondered what exactly their role as Christian leaders should be.

My understanding of the connections between shepherding, pastoral care, and leadership has been shaped by Ezekiel 34. God asks Ezekiel to prophesy against the shepherds of Israel who have been feeding themselves rather than the sheep. "You have not strengthened the weak, you have not healed the sick, you have not bound up the injured, you have not brought back the strayed, you have not sought the lost" (verse 4).

Because the human shepherds have failed so profoundly, God says, "I myself will search for my sheep. . . . I will feed them with good pasture. . . . I myself will be the shepherd of my sheep. . . . I will seek the lost, and I will bring back the strayed, and I will bind up the injured, and I will strengthen the weak" (verses 11–16).

These are astonishingly tender and nurturing tasks for a leader to perform, and they are rooted in the character of God who cares deeply for each person. When we engage in Christian pastoral care, we stand in a long line of leaders and carers who go back to Jesus, the Good Shepherd, whose sheep rely on him for safety and follow him because they know his voice (John 10:4, 9). And Jesus, in using those words, was reflecting a heritage that went even further back, to an understanding of God, the Shepherd of Israel, who called leaders to engage in the kinds of caring that shepherds did.

I have found it enlightening to compare the tasks of the shepherd from Ezekiel 34 to the seven verbs related to pastoral care:

Be shepherds of God's flock that is under your care, watching over them—not because you must, but because you are willing, as God wants you to be.

—1 Peter 5:2 NIV

healing, sustaining, guiding, reconciling, nurturing, liberating, and empowering. All of those seven actions connect in one way or another with the role of the shepherd. How can pastoral carers engage in those seven forms of care in a way that reflects this Shepherd God?

God Is Present

Shepherds, in order to do their work, have to be present with the sheep, and the term "ministry of presence" is often used to describe an important aspect of pastoral care. I have had two "aha" moments related to pastoral care and the ministry of presence.

The first came twenty-five years ago when I attended a "mini-CPE" course. I had graduated from seminary without taking Clinical Pastoral Education (CPE), which was recommended but not required for my degree. At that time, CPE was a primary means of training for pastoral care, and I couldn't work it into my schedule as a seminary student.

One of my closest friends had taken CPE, and she described it to me in detail. For the ten weeks of the course, she worked full time as a hospital chaplain. Every week she had to write up numerous "verbatims," which were scripts of conversations she had with patients, and she brought the verbatims to meetings with the other students and their supervisor.

The goal in discussing the verbatims was to understand what was going on inside her when she talked with people, so that she could be aware of the inner forces that had an impact on what she said or didn't say to patients. My friend found CPE to be grueling, demanding, and enlightening.

When I heard that a mini-CPE course was going to be offered in Seattle, a one-week version of the much longer formal course, I eagerly signed up. In the group of about fifteen, I was a very active participant in the discussion about how to help people.

Yes!

> When it comes to pastoral care, my experience has been that ministers easily lose sight of the distinctiveness of care that unfolds against the backdrop of the Christian story. That is, they lose sight of what it is they have to bring to the caregiving party that other (professional) caregivers do not—which is to say ministers let go of their distinctive vocation and training.
>
> —Allan H. Cole, "What Makes Care Pastoral?"[1]

At some point in the conversation, I was stunned by what the instructors were trying to say. God, they said, dwells inside every Christian. By the power of the Holy Spirit living inside us, whenever we enter into any situation, we bring God's presence into that situation, and sometimes God's presence is all that's needed. Advice, helpful ideas, and strategies—all of which come all too easily to me in conversations—are appropriate sometimes, but many times simply being with someone in pain is all that's necessary.

They used the term "ministry of presence" to describe this reality, and it was a totally new and revolutionary idea for me. This notion of a ministry of presence helped me to cut back on my tendency to talk too much, and I began to try to curb my knee-jerk tendency to give advice.

My second "aha" moment related to pastoral care came fifteen years later in a seminar by two chaplains I had never met before. They talked about the ministry of presence, and in the discussion afterwards, I told the story of my experience at that mini-CPE course. One of the chaplains, whom I later grew to know and respect deeply, said to me in a gentle tone, "Lynne, when you come into a situation, you don't bring God's presence with you. God is already there."

The biblical undergirding for the ministry of presence goes back to the presence of God witnessed to in the Hebrew Scriptures. God, who was already present with Abraham, guided him to leave his homeland (Gen 12:1). God was present to Moses in the burning bush (Exod 3:1–15).

After Moses died, God said to Joshua, "As I was with Moses, so I will be with you; I will not fail you or forsake you" (Josh 1:5). God guided David, Esther, Josiah, Ruth, and many other individuals and groups of people. The psalmist describes God as Shepherd, and Ezekiel recounts God's word to the people of Israel that God will be their shepherd. Where are shepherds? They stay close to the sheep.

This sense of God's presence with the people of God comes to its fruition and fullness in the incarnation, a key biblical and theological foundation for the ministry of presence in pastoral care. God comes ✓ to broken, hurting, and sinful people in Jesus Christ.

Jesus's Presence

Jesus had long interactions with people on the margins of Jewish life, such as the woman at the well (John 4), as well as people at the heart of the Jewish hierarchy like Jairus, a synagogue ruler (Mark 5:21–43). Jesus talked to a Roman centurion (Matt 8:5–13) and a gentile woman (Matt 15:21–28). Jesus was present to and with a variety of people, giving support, challenge, healing, wisdom, and the kingdom of God.

Henry Covert, a former police officer and prison chaplain, lists characteristics of the ministry of presence as exemplified by Jesus:

> Where can I go from your spirit?
> Or where can I flee from your presence?
> If I ascend to heaven, you are there;
> if I make my bed in Sheol, you are there.
> If I take the wings of the morning
> and settle at the farthest limits of the sea,
> even there your hand shall lead me,
> and your right hand shall hold me fast.
>
> —Psalm 139:7–10

He noticed, sought out those in need.
He stopped.
He was horrified.
He was angry.
He loved.
He loved widely, yet personally.
He healed relevantly.
He crossed lines.
He healed as a servant.[2]

These responses are quite wide-ranging and may expand possibilities for carers who want to think as broadly as possible about what a ministry of presence might look like in practice.

Covert emphasizes the significance of the suffering and forsakenness of Jesus for people who are incarcerated. Prison chaplains and other carers, Covert says, convey to prisoners a sense of God's presence with the forsaken because of Jesus's own experience of forsakenness.[4]

Covert's words are relevant to all who provide care for people who are suffering:

> Christian ministry must be an intentional and sensitive presence that makes a difference through caring and the willingness to share and expose itself. The involvement of the church is not exercised from a distance or in an obligatory way, but through a love that seeks out human need and suffering.[5]

Ultimately, Covert argues that the ministry of presence is summed up by compassion.[6]

Experiencing God's Presence

Experiencing God's presence in pastoral care settings is sometimes relatively easy. Imagine that Susan wants to grow in praying for her children and her role as mother, and I brainstorm with her about it. Both of us are committed Christians, and both of us think prayer

God's presence is at his own initiative, involving extreme sacrifice. The same ministry of initiative and sacrifice belongs to the church.

—Henry Covert, *Ministry to the Incarcerated*[3]

matters. God feels present in our conversation and when we pray together.

What about a situation where the care recipient has been a person of faith but currently feels abandoned by God? In what way is God present in that conversation? How should the pastoral carer talk about God? Things get even more complicated when care recipients have no faith in God at all or are perhaps antagonistic to the idea of God.

I taught a course on Christian chaplaincy several times. My students discussed with great energy the question of the ministry of presence in settings where the other people are not believers or are hostile to God for some reason.

Some of my students have a clear passion for and gifts in evangelism, and they were adamant that their highest priority as a caregiver should be to open up possibilities for exploration of faith. They argued that people are created for relationship with God, and therefore to exercise compassion is to make space to discuss God. They expressed their awareness that sensitivity and careful listening are required.

They had no desire to turn a person in pain away from God by being too pushy, but they strongly believed that ultimately our only hope is faith in Christ, and they wanted to create conversations where faith can be explored.

Other students were equally adamant that being physically and emotionally present to others is Christians' central calling, without necessarily mentioning God at all, knowing God's Spirit is already at work in the situation. If the care recipient wants to talk about God, Jesus, prayer, the Bible, or other topics related to faith, these students knew they needed to be willing and prepared to do so.

However, they argued fervently that in this secular world, where so many interactions involve contact with people who are atheists, agnostics, or people who follow other religions or other spiritual paths, our first commitment must be to show respect, honor, and compassion for other people as we are present with them. We are, they said, Christian carers who believe God's presence is in us and with us, and we show forth that presence by the quality of our love and compassion, not with words about God.

Despite these conflicting views, most of my students liked an article about the ministry of presence by Neil Holm, an Australian seminary professor. He argues that "believers are meant to live their lives in the presence of God and this relationship with God is the foundation for relationships with others."[8]

Holm observes that people can be physically present with others without paying much attention to the other person's reality or God's presence in the encounter. The goal with the ministry of presence is to pay attention to the deeper realities in each encounter.

Holm notes that the Holy Spirit opens our eyes to God's presence with us, and we depend on the Holy Spirit for that awareness.[9] The ministry of presence, then, is strongly Trinitarian. We understand from the Hebrew Scriptures that God is present with the people of God as a Shepherd, the One who strengthens, heals, guides, feeds, and seeks the lost.

We see the fullness of this presence in the life, suffering, death, and resurrection of Jesus, the One who enters with us into brokenness and forsakenness. God dwells in us through the Holy Spirit, the One who brings us an awareness of the blessed presence of the Triune God.

> Christians have no monopoly on the use of the term "pastoral care." Some would not want it anyway. In *Learning to Care*, Michael Taylor, for example, distinguishes between pastoral care and Christian pastoral care. The former consists of any helping act done by any person, whereas the latter consists of acts undertaken by Christians. Many people apart from Taylor would want to affirm the enormous value of any kind of caring act, no matter who performs it. Some would see this as doing the will of God, even if God is not the recognized motivator or enabler.
>
> —Stephen Pattison, *A Critique of Pastoral Care*[7]

In recent years, theologians have written a great deal about the communal nature of the Trinity.[10] They argue that humans are created in the image of a relational God. Understanding pastoral care as grounded in the social Trinity illuminates the relational nature of pastoral care. In our time, we often engage in pastoral care in teams (addressed in chapter 2). We try to connect people to communities. We understand that people are embedded in a network of relationships, and pastoral care needs to take those relationships into account (addressed in chapter 7). The God who is present with us is a God of relationships.

Uniquely Christian Pastoral Care

God is our Shepherd. We experience God's loving and compassionate presence with us through the incarnation of Jesus and the sending of the Holy Spirit. The communal nature of the Trinity shapes our relationships with others. These are some of the key theological and biblical principles that undergird Christian pastoral care.

In our time, when pastoral care interactions increasingly involve being present with people who do not share our faith commitment, and when the term "pastoral care" is sometimes applied to the kinds of care provided in secular settings by school counselors and employee assistance program therapists, Christian carers must be clear in their own minds about the unique aspects of Christian pastoral care.

Tim Farabaugh, a Methodist minister and nursing home CEO, expresses my own perspective on Christian pastoral care and the ministry of presence:

> By our presence and by our attitudes, we communicate our own experience of the love and compassion of God in Jesus Christ. By such a presence with others, we witness to our knowledge of God's love. This is what Christians do. We witness to the redeeming love of Jesus Christ.[11]

The communal nature of the Trinity shapes our relationships with others.

Farabaugh emphasizes presence and attitudes as the central forms of communication, which feels comfortable to me, someone who is not at all gifted in evangelism. Yet the word "witness" leaves a lot of room for interpretation.

We can testify or witness to God's love and compassion in Jesus in many ways, through actions, attitudes, or words, whichever is appropriate at the time. Even though I am much more comfortable witnessing to God's love through careful listening in conversations with people who are not Christians, there are times God calls me to speak about the redeeming love of Jesus Christ, and I need to be open to those times.

The only thing I would want to add to Farabaugh's words is the idea that pastoral care happens communally. The best Christian pastoral care involves communal support for both caregiver and care receiver. We experience God's presence in relationships as well as individually. Because the Triune God is a relational God, God's love is often made real in relationships.

For Reflection and Discussion

1 In what ways does the shepherd imagery in the Bible speak to you about core values for pastoral care?

2 Ponder the incarnation and the pattern of Jesus's ministry described in the Gospels. Which incidents do you resonate with as models for pastoral care today? What aspects of Jesus's ministry ← make you the most uncomfortable?

3 What do the words "ministry of presence" evoke for you? In what ways have you experienced God's presence when people ← have been present with you and for you?

④ For you, what are the unique components that Christians bring to pastoral care? Write a prayer for yourself as a Christian pastoral carer, drawing on the image of God the Shepherd, Jesus the Good Shepherd and Incarnate One, or other theological and biblical principles.

For Further Reading

Stone, Howard. *Theological Context for Pastoral Caregiving: Word in Deed.* London: Routledge, 1996.

> This book draws on the author's clinical practice of pastoral care and counseling to illustrate theological foundations and themes for pastoral care.

4

Christian Pastoral Care Is Missional

Personal charisma ?

RENEE ENJOYS almost every component of being a minister. Her favorite aspect, among the many tasks she finds energizing, is pastoral care. She enjoys most hospital visits, especially meeting extended family members and hearing a bit of their stories. Weddings and funerals also give her the opportunity to meet members of extended families.

The congregation she serves is in a town of fourteen thousand, so she often encounters these family members in shops, at Rotary Club, and when she goes on walks. She has listened to many people's stories about why they no longer attend church. She has heard lots of reasons for drifting away from church or choosing to do something else on Sunday mornings.

After a couple of years serving in her town, Renee found that some of the family members she met at weddings and funerals and in hospital rooms started to show up on Sunday morning at her church. They had met her, they felt accepted by her, and they were curious about what she might be like as a minister. Many of those visitors have stayed.

Renee has served this congregation for six years, and the congregation has enjoyed slow and steady growth over those years. Renee would never claim credit for that growth. As an observer, however, I can see that Renee's commitment to pastoral care, and the way she engages in it, has been missional, even though she would not use that word.

What Does Missional Mean?

The word "missional" began to appear in books and articles in the 1990s. The idea is rooted in two similar verses in the Gospel of John. In his prayer for his disciples and for future disciples, Jesus prays, "As you have sent me into the world, so I have sent them into the world" (John 17:18; see also John 20:21).

[handwritten note in left margin: Why not "Great Commission"?]

[handwritten note in margin: missional = for a message]

The Latin word for "send" is *missio*, used in early translations of the New Testament into Latin, and we get our words "mission" and "missionary" from that word. "Missional" is simply an adjective related to "mission," just as "fictional" relates to "fiction."

Christians have always believed that we are being transformed into the image of Jesus (see 2 Cor 3:18), but in recent centuries the idea that all Christians are sent into the world as Jesus was sent has lost its prominence. Yes, of course, we have had missionaries, people with a special call to go and make the Gospel known in foreign and distant places, but many Christians have viewed mission as something they supported with money and prayer, not with their own pattern of life.

With the increasing secularization of Western culture and the growing number of people who profess no faith commitment, the notion that the church is a missionary community in its own setting has become more significant. A number of books and articles help Christians adapt to this new setting in which all Christians must be missionaries.

> You go nowhere by accident. Wherever you go, God is sending you there. Wherever you are, God has put you there. He has a purpose in your being there. Christ, who indwells in you, has something He wants to do through you, wherever you are. Believe this, and go in His grace, and love and power. Amen.
>
> —Rev. Dr. Richard C. Halverson's Benediction, US Senate Chaplain (1981–94)[1]

The Mission of God

A term that is frequently used in the missional church literature is *missio Dei*, the mission of God. The missional church writers argue that God's mission is not something to be embraced as a task. They are adamant that this perspective is not a program or series of events, nor is it a new form of the church growth movement. What, then, is it?

Alan Hirsh, the author of many books on the missional church, argues that "a proper understanding of missional begins with recovering a missionary understanding of God."[2] He believes that adopting this point of view "represents a significant shift in the way we think about church. As the people of a missionary God, we ought to engage the world the same way He does—by *going* out rather than just *reaching* out."[3] Going out requires movement into neighborhoods and gathering places where people live, work, spend time, and experience joy and pain.

Graham Hill, former church planter and now the vice principal of a theological college, gives a broad perspective on the mission of God when he suggests that

> mission is not just the conversion of the individual, nor just obedience to the word of the Lord, nor just the obligation to gather the church. It is the taking part in the sending of the Son, the *missio Dei*, with the holistic aim of establishing Christ's rule over all redeemed creation.[4]

Pastoral care is one way we participate in the ministry of the Son and engage in holistic ministry that addresses the physical, emotional, and spiritual needs of human beings both inside and outside the family of faith.

The Incarnation

A missional approach to ministry is rooted in an understanding that God cares for all people and sent Jesus into the world where hurting people live. Alan Roxburgh and Fred Romanuk, who have written widely about the missional church, stress the sending of Jesus into our world. They note:

> Missional leaders take the Incarnation of Jesus with the utmost seriousness. More than just a doctrine to be confessed, it is the key to understanding all God's activities with, through, in, and among us. It points toward an answer to the question of where God is to be found. In the Incarnation we discern that God is always to be found in what appears to be the most godforsaken of places—the most inauspicious of locations, people and situations.[5]

One of my favorite books on the missional church uses the word "sentness" to describe a missional stance for ministry.[6] We are sent like Jesus was sent, and what we will find in "godforsaken" places is that the Sent One, who sends us, is already there. This commitment to "sentness" helps us meet God and serve God outside the walls of our church buildings and our homes.

In the previous chapter, I described my "aha" moments related to God's presence in me and with me as I serve, and my realization that God is already present before I enter any situation. The incarnation of Jesus—God with us in all situations, God with all people, including those on the margins—lies behind a commitment to "sentness" as foundational for Christian living, to serve and be sent as Jesus was. This approach shapes pastoral care in our time.

Missional Patterns of Pastoral Care

Renee's pattern of ministry, described above, is motivated by the love of Jesus and her own love for people. That love sends her with joy into hospital rooms, funeral homes, and Rotary Club meetings. There she meets people outside her congregation and listens to their stories of church, faith, God, spirituality—and often the absence of those things—and the connections with their everyday lives.

Another example of missional service comes from a congregation I've visited, located next door to an elementary school. The leaders of the congregation decided they should try to build connections with the school, so the minister and a couple of lay leaders went to talk with the principal. The visitors from the church suggested that perhaps church members could do tutoring.

The principal seemed hesitant, so they asked if there was something else they could help with. His response: "Yes, what we need most is help with head lice." Congregation members received training from a nurse in how to help parents deal with head lice, and for several years the congregation has supported the school in this way.

Relationships have formed between church members and parents. They share stories, and some of those stories relate to the spiritual journeys of the parents. Because of those relationships, the church was able to start a weekly after-school program that many kids from families who do not attend church participate in. This nurtures even more relationships between parents and church members, allowing for conversations about life, faith, and spiritual commitments.

In another congregation located in a low-income neighborhood, the leaders did some informal research about the needs of people in their community. Those who were out of work had difficulty going to job interviews because they lacked the right clothes for the interviews. The church set up a clothing bank where job seekers could borrow the appropriate clothing.

The clothes functioned as a bridge for relationships, and congregation members grew in their connections with people in the wider community and learned of more needs. After some time, the congregation then began to offer seminars on how to put one's best self forward in job interviews.

Another congregation housed a food bank that was open in the late afternoon one day a week. The leaders of the congregation decided to start hosting an open dinner on the same evening, so food-bank patrons could sit down for a meal with congregation members. In the two decades that the dinner has been running, congregation members have continually been encouraged to attend the dinner

> The Spirit of the Lord is upon me,
>   because he has anointed me
>   to bring good news to the poor.
> He has sent me to proclaim release to the captives
>   and recovery of sight to the blind,
>   to let the oppressed go free,
> to proclaim the year of the Lord's favor.
>
> —Luke 4:18–19, Jesus quoting Isaiah 61:1–2

is this necessary?

to form relationships with the food-bank patrons and others who come to the dinner. The dinner is held in the church building, to be sure, but the invitation extends far and wide, and many homeless people attend regularly. The dinner has provided a place for relationships to form across socioeconomic boundaries, which has facilitated much pastoral care.

Pastoral care involves healing, sustaining, guiding, reconciling, nurturing, liberating, and empowering. These actions happen in conversations and relationships, and the examples I've given illustrate the variety of places inside and outside of churches where such conversations and relationships can happen. More examples are presented in chapter 7, where I discuss the webs of relationships pastoral carers must consider. Members of congregations are sent into the world as Jesus was sent, and the actions of pastoral care reflect Jesus's priorities.

Chaplaincy as Missional Ministry

Chaplaincy presents another example of the significance of a missional attitude in pastoral care. I mentioned earlier that I taught a course on chaplaincy several times. I began teaching it because of a need expressed by students. I had never been a chaplain and knew very little about it, so I began reading everything I could find by and about chaplains. In addition, I interviewed chaplains who worked in a variety of settings. I recorded the interviews and asked my students to listen to them and engage in online discussions about what they heard.

Each time I taught the class, I tried to find new readings, and I talked with more chaplains. The more I learned about chaplaincy, the more I became convinced it is a quintessential missional ministry for our time. Christian chaplains are invited to bring a faith presence into many secular settings, such as hospitals, nursing homes, hospices, prisons, the military, high schools, and universities.

In their best moments, chaplains embody the ministry of presence, watching for the ways God is already present in the situations they enter. Chaplains listen, care, and connect people with resources. Chaplains generally have no agenda to get people through the doors of a church on Sunday morning, although they rejoice whenever individuals grow closer to God in any way. Chaplaincy is an excellent paradigm for missional ministry, because chaplains leave their congregations, enter secular institutions, and provide care no matter how the care recipients respond.

Chaplaincy, with its a missional outlook on pastoral care, contrasts with the 1989 movie *Field of Dreams*. The movie told the story of a man who built a baseball field in the middle of a rural cornfield. He was responding to a strong inner message: "If you build it, they will come." This has been the working philosophy and practice of the Christian church in the West for many generations, and this approach is obviously no longer working with respect to Sunday morning worship.

However, many congregations have a significant resource in their property and buildings. When they share that resource in ways that meet specific needs in the community, people do come through the doors for such activities as Alcoholics Anonymous, holiday music events, and seminars on debt management, parenting, and other timely topics. To act missionally must involve going into the community. Needs discovered there might be met in the church building or on the church grounds, two resources many congregations can offer their communities.

> Jesus's personal welcome and his constant invitation for people to engage with the gospel he preached provide our model for pastoral care in a secular world. Our congregations may grow as a result, and they may not.

The temptation in adopting a missional approach to ministry is to believe this new perspective will "work" in the sense of increasing attendance at worship services and contributions to the church budget. However, in a secular world, Christians are called to be witnesses through their caring, words, and deeds, whether or not any measurable growth occurs for the congregation.

In Renee's case, her loving engagement with people beyond the church indeed "worked" in the area of church growth. A missional approach to pastoral care motivates members of congregations to engage in caring both inside and outside congregations as God leads them, whatever the benefit to the congregation itself. This form of engagement is modeled after Jesus, who ministered to Jews and gentiles, women and men, synagogue leaders and prostitutes.

Christians are called to be witnesses through their caring, words, and deeds, whether or not any measurable growth occurs for the congregation.

How We See Jesus

I've noticed an interesting pattern among people who desire to take the mission of God seriously. How they view Jesus's ministry affects the way they view their call to go into the world like Jesus did. Those who see Jesus primarily as one who proclaimed the gospel are usually quite motivated in the area of evangelism. Those who love the stories in the Gospels about Jesus interacting with the marginalized often feel passionate about connecting with people who are marginalized today.

Some Christians focus on Jesus as a great teacher, and they often feel called to teach or impart knowledge through teaching, speaking, writing, podcasts, videos, or other means. Those who appreciate Jesus's prophetic words to the powerful people of his time often want to engage with others around social-justice issues. This variety of ways of perceiving Jesus's ministry and creating ministries that mirror aspects of it creates a rich tapestry of forms of Christian service.

Only a very large congregation can host a weekly dinner, a clothing bank, and a community garden and send a team of people into a local school to help with head lice. Most congregations must depend on God's leadership as they discern what to undertake. Our ministry must be based in following God's guidance in imitating the model of Jesus. Spiritual practices that involve listening to God for guidance—individually and communally—are essential for living out this missional attitude.

The four skills for pastoral care discussed in the second half of this book undergird a missional approach to ministry:

- Understanding patterns and implications of stress help pastoral carers ask good questions and perceive patterns of pain so needs can be addressed.
- Listening skills are essential in order to pay attention to what's going on in the wider community.
- Spiritual practices such as forms of prayer that enable listening to God help carers to listen for God's guidance about when and where to be involved, and Bible study helps carers learn about God's purposes and the model of Jesus.
- Ways of acting and thinking that nurture resilience are essential for carers with a desire for missional service in the wider community, because the needs can be overwhelming.

Training Tips

If you lead training sessions for pastoral carers,

1 Allow time for carers to articulate their understanding of the mission of God in a way that is helpful for them.

2 Discuss the ways that Jesus's ministry is a model for Christian pastoral carers today.

3 Discuss examples of pastoral care beyond the congregation from this chapter, your own congregation, and other congregations participants know about. Allow space for participants to ponder ways God is calling them to provide care outside your congregation.

We are invited by the missional church authors—and also by the New Testament—to embrace a missional perspective, because it comes from the heart of God and is modeled by the ministry of Jesus. Alan Roxburgh, one of my favorite missional church writers, argues that we are called to consider who God is and what God is doing and then to "join God's life in the world."[7]

Joining God's life in the world will always involve pastoral care, because human beings who live in our broken world always need care. Sometimes the pastoral care arises from church ministries in the community, and other times pastoral care needs nudge congregations to create ministries. Either way, many of the actions of pastoral care in the twenty-first century are missional.

This goes back to outdated def. of pastoral care to "troubled people"

For Reflection and Discussion

1 Whether the term "missional" is familiar or new to you, when you ponder the invitation to participate in God's mission, what emotions do you feel?

2 How would you describe the mission of God? If someone asked you why Jesus came to earth and what Jesus came to do, how would you respond?

3 What are the connections between your understanding of God's mission and your own ministry, your involvement in small groups, or your caring relationships in other settings?

4 What do you find most significant about Jesus's ministry? Write a prayer for yourself as a carer who wants to model yourself after Jesus's incarnation.

Resources

Rouse, Rick. *Beyond Church Walls: Cultivating a Culture of Care.* Minneapolis: Fortress Press, 2016.

Rouse unites a missional approach with a concern for pastoral care in the communities beyond the walls of the church, paralleling the concerns of this chapter and chapter 7.

Sparks, Paul, Tim Soerens, and Dwight J. Friesen. *The New Parish: How Neighborhood Churches Are Transforming Mission, Discipleship and Community.* Downers Grove, IL: InterVarsity, 2014.

A call for Christians and congregations to be re-rooted in their local communities, including care, activism, and paying attention to the good things already going on.

Roxburgh, Alan. *Joining God, Remaking Church, Changing the World: The New Shape of the Church in Our Time.* New York: Morehouse, 2015.

An accessible book by my favorite of the missional church writers. Roxburgh gives history and theological perspective with concrete illustrations of the church going into the neighborhood.

5
Pastoral Care Occurs across Ethnicities and Religions

FAMILIES ARE increasingly diverse. My own extended family illustrates this trend. In the year 2000, every one of my extended family members was white, and we were pretty traditional. Since then, our younger son told us he is gay, our older son married a Japanese woman, a great-niece married an African American man, and a cousin also married an African American.

Another cousin, one of our closest friends, adopted a Guatemalan baby with a significant Mayan heritage. At our son's wedding reception in Seattle, I watched several of the guests from Japan as they passed around the newly adopted baby boy from Guatemala. When I saw this juxtaposition of cultures, I thought, "This is life in America today."

More than a dozen years have passed since that wedding where the Japanese guests had such a good time with a Guatemalan baby. That baby is now an adolescent, with white parents who have done all they can to nurture his connections with Guatemalan culture and his birth family there. Our wonderful Japanese daughter-in-law speaks only Japanese to our beloved granddaughter, so that our granddaughter is able to communicate with her Japanese relatives. The Guatemalan American teenager (fluent in Spanish) and the young Japanese American girl (fluent in Japanese) are second cousins, and they are fond of each other.

My family is not unique. In most congregations, pastoral carers will hear stories like these. In addition, workplaces are increasingly diverse. Cross-cultural challenges are a part of everyday life for a growing number of people in our congregations, and they talk about those challenges in pastoral care settings.

Imagine that my husband and I died together in an accident. Whoever conducted our funeral service would have to explain parts of the service to our Japanese daughter-in-law, who was raised Buddhist and knows little about the Christian tradition. The days when most extended families and workplaces were composed of people of the same ethnicity and religion are long past.

The Challenge of Vocabulary

People have vastly different ethnic origins and ancestral histories, and finding vocabulary to talk about these differences is challenging. In the United States, the words "race," "multiracial," and "racism" frequently appear in these discussions. These words are imprecise because they clump together very diverse people, such as Filipinos and people from India—whose countries of origin are thousands of miles apart—into one category, Asian. In addition, many scholars argue that race is a social construct with no basis in biology.[1]

It might seem that the word "culture" would be a better way to describe some of the differences between people who now live in the United States but have roots in different countries like Guatemala and Japan. However, Methodist minister and evangelist Stephen Rhodes, in his book on the church in a multiethnic world, notes that culture is very difficult to define.

Rhodes writes about culture as systems of beliefs, values, and customs. He also describes culture as a kind of mental road map.[2] He cites British theologian Lesslie Newbigin's definition of culture as "the sum total of ways of living developed by a group of human beings and handed on from generation to generation."[3]

People live within multiple cultures. I am a white woman, an American, a Seattleite, a Christian, a Presbyterian, and I hold advanced academic degrees. All of these areas of my life have

> After this I looked, and there was a great multitude that no one could count, from every nation, from all tribes and people and languages, standing before the throne and before the Lamb.
>
> —Revelation 7:9

↓

A legitimate question to ask is whether all persons are multicultural persons, with many different symbol systems or cultural worldviews operative within each individual.

—David Pearson, "Crossing Ethnic Thresholds: Multiculturalisms in Comparative Perspective"[4]

3 options?
· race
· culture
· ethnicity

embedded me in cultures that have shaped me. In addition, I have lived overseas for more than a quarter of my life, and I have been influenced by those places as well. The word "culture" is frustratingly broad when used to describe all these influences.

yes!

Right now in America, the word "race" evokes conflict. "Culture" refers not just to ethnic origins but also to so many other groups of people who have influenced us. Along with some scholars, I prefer the word "ethnicity" when I refer to the ancestral origins that influence the way we live. Part of my motivation comes from the Greek word *ethnos*, used more than 150 times in the New Testament to refer to people from different nations or kinship groups, united by culture and common traditions.

As I have talked with ministers of multiethnic congregations, I have heard a diversity of vocabulary. One minister, who is married to a woman from another country, uses the terms "multicultural" and "intercultural" to describe patterns he observes in congregations. He argues that the presence of multiple ethnicities makes a community multicultural, but only deep relationships across cultures makes a community intercultural.

good!

He said that a few years ago he looked at his congregation and observed,

> We had become multicultural. That's fine, but multicultural to my mind is not actually the Gospel. The Gospel is intercultural. So we had wound up with a church where we could all come in, whoever we were, and there would be buddies who looked like us. There might only be four, because we're not a big church, but the white guys could stand in the corner talking to each other, and the Singaporean guys, and there's enough South African Colored guys. Instead of having the cliques, interculturalism is when some of my friends *don't* look like me. And that's a deeper level which takes a deeper level of engagement. So currently we're really in that process of rethinking that and developing a new set of strategies for moving from multicultural to intercultural.

This minister has a desire to create spaces characterized by a sense of belonging for everyone. Within his own congregation, he has promoted language to describe his desire. For people outside his congregation, the language may be confusing when used without explanation.

Outside the United States, "multicultural" and "multiculturalism" can evoke a variety of ideas. Jonathan Chaplin, former director of a British institute for Christian ethics, notes six different ways "multiculturalism" is spoken of in various settings in the United Kingdom: "a fact of cultural diversity, a fact of religious diversity, a doctrine of multi-faithism, an assumption of cultural relativism, a principle of public policy toward minorities, a cause of segregation."[5]

The lack of precision in all of these terms and the wide diversity in the way they are used can be quite frustrating. This lack of precision, while irritating and sometimes confusing, must be acknowledged, but must not stop us from talking about the different gifts and challenges brought to congregations by people from wildly different countries and origins.

On pastoral care teams, we must discuss challenges and opportunities that arise from the presence of people of diverse ethnicities in our congregations and neighborhoods. It may also be wise to spend some time talking about the vocabulary you use and what it means in your setting.

Challenges from Migration

Pastoral care challenges related to ethnic diversity arise in part from migration. The world is on the move. Daniel Groody, a Roman Catholic theologian who writes about theology of migration, noted in 2009 that the number of migrants worldwide had doubled in the previous twenty-five years from one hundred million to nearly two hundred million people. One person in thirty-five worldwide does not live in their country of birth, a number greater than the population of Brazil.[6]

Many countries have experienced an increase in migration in recent years. In the United States, 13 percent of residents were born overseas. In the United Kingdom, that figure is 12 percent, for Canada 20 percent, New Zealand 25 percent, and Australia 27 percent.[8] Those percentages do not include second-generation immigrants who were born in the country to which their parents migrated. Second-generation immigrants have specific challenges unique to their situation, as they navigate their parents' culture of origin as well as the culture of their birth.

Multi Cultural competence

Paul Kivel's 27?

Seminary professor Charles van Engen argues, "We are all being radically impacted by the largest redistribution of people the globe has ever seen."[7] In most cities and towns worldwide, increasing diversity is visible in neighborhoods, workplaces, extended families, and congregations. The diversity often involves both culture and religion.

Several of the pastoral care skills described in part 2 of this book take on particular significance because of migration, especially understanding stress and listening skills. Imagine a pastoral care conversation in the United States with someone who looks Asian. That person might be a migrant, and careful listening can help tease out which aspects of the birth culture are still significant to that person. Of course, someone who looks Asian could also be a third- or fourth-generation migrant who feels strongly identified with American culture.

In between are second-generation migrants with their specific challenges. Increasingly common is the term "1.5 generation" to describe people who migrated with their parents between the ages of five and fifteen. Many members of the 1.5 generation usually speak both their parents' and their adopted country's languages fluently, yet they don't identify with the new culture as fully as second- or third-generation migrants.

Not just a trait of migrants

Two migration researchers, Peggy Levitt and B. Nada Jaworsky, use the term "fluid spaces" to describe the fact that migrants' experiences constantly shift. They write that recent scholarship "understands transnational migration as taking place within fluid social spaces that are constantly reworked through migrants' simultaneous embeddedness in more than one society."[9]

A man who pastors a multiethnic Baptist church in Auckland affirmed the significance of the shifting and fluid experience of migrants. He told me about an Indian man who moved to New Zealand. This migrant from India longed to learn more about his new country, and he desired to make friends with Kiwis and other migrants to New Zealand, so he began to attend the multiethnic Baptist congregation. After a few years, the man's father died, and the man moved to an Indian migrant congregation, because he needed the embrace of his own culture as he mourned.

The fluidity mentioned by Levitt and Jaworsky illuminates the reality that most migrants continue to value some aspects of their home culture, while embracing aspects of their new culture. My own experience living for a decade in New Zealand illustrates this complexity. I appreciate the New Zealand emphasis on "a fair go." Fairness has much higher value in New Zealand than in the United States, and I love it. At the same time, I value the forthright conversation common in the United States, while New Zealanders tend to be more reserved.

These are only two small examples of the way I occupied a "fluid space" while living in New Zealand. Pastoral carers need to be aware that migrants will want to keep aspects of their own cultures of origin and to adopt aspects of their new culture. The energy necessary to navigate this reality is one of the underlying, continual stressors on migrants, and pastoral carers need to be aware of this stress and listen for it.

NAÏVE

In the past, the words "immigrant" and "emigrant" were often used when discussing migration. An immigrant is someone coming to a new country and an emigrant designates someone leaving a country. More often today the word "migrant" is used to represent a new reality: people increasingly move back and forth between their country of origin and other countries.

While increased migration presents a diversity challenge for pastoral carers, a second challenge comes from diversity issues that have been a part of life in many countries for decades or centuries. In the United States, Canada, Australia, and New Zealand, indigenous people have experienced marginalization in many ways. In some cases, learning to serve migrants has helped Christians in these countries care more deeply for their indigenous peoples.

The United States also has long-standing issues between whites and African Americans that seem to have become more intense, or at least more visible, in recent years. The UK deals with diversity issues between English, Irish, Welsh, and Scottish people, and Canadians are always aware of challenges in the relationship between French-speaking and English-speaking citizens.

Facing the challenges of ministry in a world of migration has helped some American Christians grow in skills and commitment for relationships between whites and African Americans. Many of the same skills apply to relationships across all ethnicities: patient listening, openness to the other person's experience, and willingness to grow in understanding the stressors experienced by people in minority or marginalized situations.

Research on Diversity

Because of the increases in migration, a robust literature on the challenges of work and ministry in ethnically diverse settings has emerged. Three books with vividly descriptive titles, written by Christians, capture some of the challenges: *Many Colors: Cultural Intelligence for a Changing Church,*[10] *A Many Colored Kingdom: Multicultural Dynamics for Spiritual Formation,*[11] and *Ethnic Blends: Mixing Diversity into Your Local Church.*[12] This growing literature about diversity by Christians includes books and articles that discuss interfaith dialogue,[13] while the majority give practical advice to congregational leaders.

good

Daniel Groody argues that God's people have always been migrants. The nation of Israel began with God's call to Abraham to leave his homeland (Genesis 12) and continues through to Jesus who migrated from heaven to earth. Groody notes the significance of Mary, Joseph, and Jesus's flight into Egypt (Matt 2:13–15). From the beginning of his human life, Jesus experienced the dislocation of migration.[14] Pastoral carers who minister to people experiencing dislocation can highlight Jesus's identification with the challenges of migration.

The Christian books on this topic stress the significance of <u>cultural intelligence</u>, the ability to relate across cultures. They stress the value of diversity, often drawing on images from Isaiah 25:6, the heavenly banquet prepared for all peoples, and Revelation 7:9–12, where all the nations worship God together in their own languages.

Pentecost ? Tower of Babel

Many writers argue that ethnic and cultural diversity should play a role in all worship of God on earth as well as in heaven. In addition, these authors often note that in the Hebrew Scriptures, God calls the Israelites to care for migrants: "The alien who resides with you shall be to you as the citizen among you; you shall love the alien as yourself, for you were aliens in the land of Egypt: I am the Lord your God" (Lev 19:34).

Supplementing this Christian perspective on the significance of relationships across ethnicities, a growing academic literature on diversity highlights many factors relevant to carers. In a *Scientific American* article, Katherine Phillips, a professor of leadership and ethics at Columbia Business School, provides a helpful summary of research about diversity. Phillips writes:

> Decades of research by organizational scientists, psychologists, sociologists, economists and demographers show that <u>socially diverse</u> groups (that is, those with a diversity of race, ethnicity, gender and sexual orientation) <u>are more innovative than homogeneous groups.</u> It seems obvious that a group of people with diverse individual expertise would be better than a homogeneous group at solving complex, nonroutine problems. It is less obvious that social diversity should work in the same way—yet the science shows that it does.[15]

duh!

Phillips goes on to say that working with people from different backgrounds forces everyone to prepare better, to watch for and consider alternative viewpoints, and to expect that reaching consensus will require significant time and effort. She notes that working in a socially diverse setting not only promotes hard work and creativity but also encourages participants to ponder alternatives even before personal interaction takes place.[16]

These realities are significant for pastoral carers navigating cultural diversity in committee meetings and board meetings. These research findings are also relevant when care recipients describe the challenges of diversity in the workplace.

Sad!

Despite the benefits of diversity in creativity and productivity for groups, research indicates that people usually feel most comfortable in homogeneous settings. After all, it takes additional effort to relate well across cultures. The academic literature about ethnically diverse congregations also reveals a strong pull toward homogeneity and illustrates clearly that those in dominant ethnic groups find it difficult to understand the needs of those in minority groups.[17]

> In our increasingly diverse world, pastoral care might include participating in celebrations of quinceañera birthday parties, Día de los Muertos, Chinese New Year, or Kwanzaa. Pastoral care may include taking into account the complex wedding practices of people from India or the unique prayer patterns among Koreans.

Some people believe the solution to these challenges lies in treating all people as equal, with ethnicity being irrelevant. This perspective is often called being "color blind." Many of the authors of the books and articles mentioned in this chapter argue that ethnic and cultural values must be discussed openly, not ignored. These authors note that when we ignore the specifics of diversity, the majority culture predominates, often without consciousness on the part of those in that majority culture.

Yes; this is problematic

Why Focus on Ethnicity?

In *Being White: Finding our Place in a Multiethnic World*, Paula Harris describes a transition she experienced from being "color blind" to becoming aware of the significance of ethnicity and what it means to people who live as minorities. Harris, a speaker and writer, grew up as a missionary kid. Her parents raised her to be color blind, which she describes as a good and loving perspective that involves ignoring skin color and looking for common traits of humanity.

She came to understand that being color blind is an inadequate goal, however, and she and her cowriter, Doug Schaupp, list six reasons why developing an appreciation for ethnicity is consistent with biblical teaching on justice and shalom. Harris and Schaupp write that colorblindness

- ignores the heart language of our ethnic minority friends;
- misses riches God intended for our blessing;
- misses who people really are at their core;
- assumes everyone is "white like me";
- makes us vulnerable to stumbling into an Acts 6 rift; and
- numbs our hearts to the suffering of our friends.[18]

This perspective parallels the academic research described earlier and has significant implications for carers. Pastoral carers need to be aware of the complex realities that come from ethnic diversity. We need to grow in appreciating the influence of ethnic origins in the

---

Training Tips

If you lead training sessions for pastoral carers,

1 Spend some time researching the demographics of your congregation and your neighborhood, town, or city.

2 Discuss the people groups who are present and the pastoral care issues that arise from the interaction between people of different ethnicities in your community.

3 Discuss challenges in communication across cultures, especially the cultures represented in your community. Explore the vocabulary used in your context, especially *race*, *culture*, and *ethnicity*, and what they mean in everyday conversation.

4 Ponder the ways the majority culture dominates in your congregation. Discuss the pastoral care issues that might arise among those in the congregation who feel like a minority.

lives of people we care for. We need to listen for the specifics of the culture of origin and its impact on the person's life today.

Yes!

Because so many cultures are communal rather than individualistic, we also need to listen for the implication of ethnic origins for groups as well as individuals. This illustrates another of the trends of pastoral care in our time, the growing understanding that individuals are embedded in communities. This trend will be discussed in chapter 7.

Humility, compassion, and slowing down enough to enable careful listening are necessary in all pastoral care settings, but especially in relating to people of diverse ethnicities. The apostle Paul gives excellent advice for those seeking to show care across cultures: "As God's chosen ones, holy and beloved, clothe yourselves with compassion, kindness, humility, meekness and patience" (Col 3:12).

For Reflection and Discussion

1. In what settings do you engage with people who come from backgrounds different from yours? What have you learned?

2. Have you seen increased diversity in your congregation or wider community? What kinds of diversity? What challenges in pastoral care have you seen that arise from it? How have you seen pastoral carers meet those challenges?

3. In what ways have you seen listening make a difference in relationships across ethnicities or other boundaries? What do you find hardest when you listen to someone of a different ethnicity?

4. How would you like to grow in relating to people across boundaries of culture, ethnicity, and other social divisions? Write a prayer for yourself as a pastoral carer across boundaries.

Resources

Johnson, Lydia F. *Drinking from the Same Well: Cross-Cultural Concerns in Pastoral Care and Counseling.* Eugene, OR: Pickwick, 2011.

Lydia Johnson is the wise and insightful person who created the curriculum that shaped the first seven chapters of this book. She has had significant pastoral care experience across cultures, and her book addresses communication, conflict, empathy, family dynamics, suffering, and healing.

Lartey, Emmanuel Y. *In Living Color: An Intercultural Approach to Pastoral Care and Counseling.* London: Jessica Kingsley, 2003.

A landmark book about pastoral care in a global, pluralistic, postcolonial, and postmodern world, including a history of pastoral care and pastoral counseling.

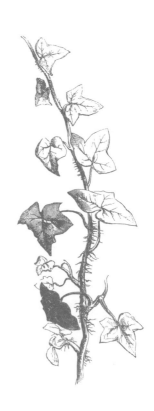

6
Pastoral Care Empowers

OUR SON, now a journalist, worked in human rights for a decade. In a blog post, he describes an incident from his teen years that shaped his perspective on his work:

> I remember talking to one of my parents' friends when I was maybe 13 or 14. She worked at a homeless shelter, she provided food and clothes and beds all winter, a big brick building in the middle of a neighborhood I had lived my whole life avoiding.
>
> I was in my Ayn Rand phase at the time, and I asked her, wasn't she worried about dependency, fraud, the homeless people going to her shelter, getting food, then going to another and getting more?
>
> "They need our help," she said. And that was it. End of sentence, end of conversation. I remember being struck by that, the simplicity of it, the clarity of genuine, actual, real-world *grace* being defined in four words right in front of me.[1]

I'm glad that our son experienced a vivid expression of grace in that woman's words. His response to her words shows the power of clear motivations for offering care that are expressed simply and with conviction.

A person doesn't have to be in an "Ayn Rand phase" to wonder about dependency, abuse, and fraud, the concerns our son raised. All of these issues must be considered in pastoral care settings. In this chapter, I will focus on empowerment, which I view as the opposite of dependency.

Empowerment is an offensive strategy against dependency

Increased Interest in Empowerment

In recent decades, writers and teachers in many areas, including pastoral care, chaplaincy, social work, and counseling, have been emphasizing empowerment in new ways. Many factors contribute to this increased interest in helping people find their own strength, including a growing awareness of the dangers of creating dependency in caring relationships.

In addition, the rise in research focused on the effectiveness of various medical and public health interventions—often called outcomes research—has affected the desire to evaluate the efficacy of various forms of ministry. My husband, a retired dentist and dental educator, remembers the late 1980s and early 1990s, when evidence-based outcomes research began to influence the practice and teaching of dentistry, as well as medicine. The effectiveness of each medical and dental procedure was evaluated weeks, months, and even years later, based on measurable outcomes.

Our son recounts an early application of evidence-based outcomes research to international development. In an article in the *New Republic*, he describes an MIT economics professor who was working in the late 1990s with an NGO in Kenya that distributed textbooks to students in poor rural villages.

This professor encouraged the NGO to set up two groups, one that would receive textbooks and one that would not. After four years of collecting data on the educational trajectory of each student, the researchers found that some of the students had improved academically and some had not, but the difference did not depend on free textbooks. On average, the students who received textbooks were not any better off than the ones who did not.[3]

This kind of research asks questions that relate to empowerment: How many of the people who received help are now more able to support their families? How many are less able to support their

> What does it mean to help? When does our help amount to hindrance? When are we getting less help—or more—than we actually want? When are we kidding ourselves in the name of helping (or of refusing to "enable") someone else?
>
> —Online editorial comments about the book *Help: The Original Human Dilemma* by Garrett Keizer[2]

families? After receiving help, how many more or fewer children are going to school? How many children are doing better at school? How many are doing worse? This quantitative research is having an impact on a generation of donors to international development projects, and millennial generation donors are particularly interested in outcomes research on development projects.[4]

Outcomes research is also influencing pastoral care. No one wants to provide care for another person or group of people in a way that doesn't help. What a waste of effort! No one wants to engage in forms of caring that actually harm people, a violation of every value that drives pastoral care. The challenges for pastoral carers related to dependency and empowerment are twofold: we now know more about the damage to care recipients when they become dependent, and we also know more about the negative impact on carers when they take too much responsibility for other people's lives. What are the characteristics of pastoral care that empowers?

Giving and Receiving

In the introduction to this volume, I gave you a glimpse of my years of depression and the kinds of care that brought me rays of hope. I wanted you to see from the beginning of the book that I am a person who needs pastoral care sometimes and gives it other times, which is true for all carers.

One of the significant trends in pastoral care today is an emphasis on its reciprocal nature. This is a somewhat invisible characteristic of the kind of pastoral care that can be empowering. Peggy Way, one of the first women to teach pastoral care in a major American seminary, explains that in the Christian community "there are no permanent roles of caregiver and care receiver."[6] Way notes:

> We now know more about the damage to care recipients when they become dependent, and we also know more about the negative impact on carers when they take too much responsibility for other people's lives.

Empowering care:
- reciprocal
- hopeful → this is not the final word – nurtures active thinking & behavior
→ 7 verbs
- limit advice
- be present w/o an agenda

In Christian theology, caregiver and care receiver are viewed as one; that is, those who offer care are also those who need to receive it, and those who receive care are gifted in offering it. . . . This not only diminishes the possibility that some groups of caregivers seem to commit the heresy that they are God; it also enriches the possibility that there are many caregivers available in ordinary congregations and in the midst of a culture overflowing with human needs.[7]

Peggy Way

→ ? implications for boundary-maintenance

The pattern of pastoral care Way describes contrasts greatly with the forms of pastoral care common a few decades ago, where the minister visited parishioners in their homes or talked with people in his office, and the minister was always the caregiver and people in the congregation were always the care receivers.

This new understanding helps carers not to view themselves as somehow immune from suffering or somehow better than the care recipient. Carers are pilgrims on a journey toward wholeness, just like the recipients. Carers who see themselves in this light are less likely to "commit the heresy that they are God."

Luke Smith → "You will never be a minister until you allow yourself to be ministered to."

Also → Learning to ask for help

Yes! Way argues that this perspective gives strength and hope to the people who are care recipients in this moment, because it assures them that some other time they might be caregivers. This encourages care recipients to find their own strength so that later they will be able to help others.

In chapter 1, I mentioned Henri Nouwen's description of caring: "The friend who can be silent with us in a moment of despair or confusion, who can stay with us in an hour of grief and bereavement, who can tolerate not-knowing, not-curing, not-healing and face with us the reality of our powerlessness, that is the friend who cares."[5] When we can enter into the powerlessness that other people feel and let them emerge from the powerlessness at their own pace, we are helping them find their own strength.

The apostle Paul, early in his second letter to the Corinthians, writes,

> Blessed be the God and Father of our Lord Jesus Christ, the Father of mercies and the God of all consolation, who consoles us in all our affliction, so that we may be able to console those who are in any affliction with the consolation with which we ourselves are consoled by God (2 Cor 1:3–4).

We console because God has consoled us. We learn how to console from the way God consoles us, using a variety of people and circumstances to show us love. We care because we have received care. This perspective enables carers to come alongside people in need in a way that reduces hierarchy and contributes to empowerment.

The reciprocal nature of all Christian caring is illustrated further by what happens in hospitality settings. Christine Pohl's 1999 book, *Making Room: Recovering Hospitality as a Christian Tradition*,[9] is one of the earliest books in a burgeoning literature about hospitality. Pohl's book influenced me to see all Christian ministry under the umbrella of hospitality, which includes this notion of reciprocity.

Many authors on hospitality point out the guest-host switch that happens in the road to Emmaus story in Luke 24:13–35. The two people walking on the road invite a stranger into their home. At the dinner table, the guest takes bread and breaks it, assuming the role of host. In that moment, the guest is revealed to be Jesus. The guest becomes the host, and the hosts are guests at his table.

Church historian Amy Oden notes, "Many early Christian texts deliberately confuse the roles of host and guest. Particularly in stories about hospitality offered, it is sometimes hard to tell who is giving and who is receiving."[10] When we host others, we can expect to meet Jesus in them, and when Jesus is at the table with us, he becomes the host.

This guest–host switch is a reality that both bemuses and blesses. When we meet Jesus in others, the privilege is ours. We see something wonderful in them that reflects Jesus's nature, and when we respond to them with respect and even awe, we are acting in ways that empower.

When I invite friends over for dinner, I'm excited to see them. I ask them about their lives. I expect to see good things in their lives, and I try to honor those strengths I see in them. Who they are, their gifts and strengths, is at the center when I exercise hospitality. In some small way, each guest becomes a host because that person brings gifts to me. When I can bring this attitude into pastoral care settings, I know I am more likely to bring hope and empowerment.

Nurturing Constructive Thinking

When carers adopt a spirit of hospitality, honoring the care recipient as a guest and looking for gifts and strengths, they help the care recipient find inner strength. This perspective, often unspoken but powerful nonetheless, conveys hope, and hope is empowering. Hope helps people think optimistically about situations and believe that solutions are possible.

When carers know deep down that they were once, or might someday be, in a situation similar to the care receiver's, they communicate that the current situation is not the final word in the care receiver's life. This also helps care recipients think optimistically about their situation.

In a section entitled "The New Shape of Pastoral Care," Howard Stone, a psychologist and emeritus professor, writes, "Pastoral care aims to help people develop not only their feelings and attitudes, but also constructive behaviors and thinking. It recognizes that what a person feels and does greatly depends on what that individual thinks and believes."[12] Helping people think and believe that resources are available within their community and within themselves nurtures their movement toward constructive behaviors and thinking.

Often, often, often goes the Christ in the stranger's guise.

—Ancient Celtic Rune of Hospitality[11]

good questions

In addition to listening carefully to care recipients talk about their desires, needs, and concerns, carers can steer conversations in the direction of constructive behaviors and thinking. Questions that help people find resources within themselves or from their faith, based on past experiences, include:

- What actions or people have helped you in the past to cope with situations like this?
- In the past, what unexpected strength did you find to deal with hard things?
- In what ways have you experienced God's help in years past with challenges like this one?

Helping people identify the positive things they have been doing in the midst of the current challenges, perhaps using questions like these, is also empowering:

- Since this difficult situation started, what have you found helpful in dealing with it?
- In recent weeks, what kinds of support have you experienced from people in your life?
- How have you been praying for this challenge? Have you seen answers to your prayers? If so, what have you experienced?

Brainstorming options for additional ways to cope can also help people move in the direction of finding their own strength:

- Who might you ask for help?
- How might you pray for this situation?
- When you look at your own personality strengths, what can you draw on in this situation?

In addition to questions like these, several other listening skills can help people find strength within themselves, drawing on their relationship with God if they are people of faith. In chapter 9, I will describe the kinds of listening skills that are essential in pastoral care, with an emphasis on skills that help people know their own power and that help carers step outside the role of rescuer.

Pastoral Care Actions

Empowerment is the last of the seven verbs cited several times in this book to describe pastoral care: healing, sustaining, guiding, reconciling, nurturing, liberating, and empowering. The other verbs also evoke aspects of empowerment as well.

When people receive healing, the presupposition is that they will receive renewed strength and energy. Sustaining implies strengthening someone for the tasks at hand. Guiding can suggest passivity, when people take no action of their own, but guiding can also involve helping someone find the right path to step out on. Nurturing suggests undergirding and strengthening. Liberating implies freeing people from the things that bind them, giving them power to live in the wholeness God intends for them.

One of the words on the list—reconciling—relates specifically to relationships. John Patton, a retired Methodist minister and seminary professor, makes a connection between empowerment and relationships:

> Recovering one's self and one's power to live and to change in the context of a relationship is what pastoral care is all about. Care is pastoral when it looks deeper than the immediate circumstances of a person's life and reminds that person that he or she is a child of God created in and for relationship.[13]

Helping people identify where God is already at work in their situation helps them find strength in their relationship with God. Patton seems to be saying that "recovering one's self and one's power to live and to change in the context of a relationship" includes helping people grow in their own faith practices and thus nurture their relationship with God. In the introductory chapter, I noted Eugene Peterson's perspective that prayer is the "connective tissue" between everyday life and Sunday worship.[14] Therefore, helping people learn to pray in new ways about their situation can be empowering because they are building new connective tissue.

> The art of visitation becomes reframing stories. Often when people's lives radically change . . . [t]hey need help to re-frame and re-vision their lives so that the road to wholeness is opened. . . . For the encounter to be effective, the ones being visited need to find a new way of seeing their situation, whether that is in relationship to the community from which they are separated or relation to their God or in seeing themselves. They need help in being unhooked from a story of loneliness and despair.
>
> —Aart M. van Beek, "A Cross-Cultural Case for Convergence in Pastoral Thinking and Training"[15]

Patton indicates that human relationships nurture a sense of self and "power to live." That's why I appreciate ministries like the new member's classes I described in chapter 1, where the goals include helping participants learn about the congregation but also help them form connections with each other. That's why pastoral care might involve gently steering someone toward a book group, a kitchen clean-up team, or a youth ministry team in order to build relationships as well as self-confidence.

Limiting Advice-Giving

I used the words "gently steering" in the previous paragraph. What is the role of giving advice when we want to empower others? This is a burning issue for me, because I love to give advice. Giving advice is my knee-jerk response in so many different conversations. I have been working on limiting my advice-giving for what feels like decades, and I am still growing and improving.

He too!

Obviously, advice is helpful sometimes, but not very often, especially when not asked for. When the person who is experiencing a challenge comes up with the idea of how to proceed, the outcome is so much better. The person is much more likely to own the solution and act on it.

Limiting advice-giving and trying to be present without an agenda are my two current strategies for empowerment of others. Or, more accurately, they are the two strategies I am working on and growing into at the moment. I suspect that in a few years, God will call me to work on other skills. Becoming a carer who strives to help people find their own strength is a learning and growing process because carers, as well as care recipients, are on a journey toward health and wholeness.

For Reflection and Discussion

1 Have you seen *experienced* forms of helping that you think have caused damage to the care recipient or the carer? If so, what have you learned from those instances?

2 In what ways do you embrace and resist the idea that all people sometimes function as carers and sometimes as care recipients?

3 In what ways have people helped you develop "constructive behaviors and thinking"? How do you try to help others develop them?

4 What strategies for empowerment do you believe God is calling you to grow in right now? Write a prayer for yourself as a carer who helps people find their own strength.

Resources

Nouwen, Henri. *The Wounded Healer: Ministry in Contemporary Society.* New York: Doubleday, 1979.

> A classic, evocative exploration of the paradoxical reality that the wounded can best bring healing to others. I have heard from so many people that this book profoundly changed their perspective on ministry.

Keizer, Garrett. *Help: The Original Human Dilemma.* San Francisco: HarperSanFrancisco, 2004.

> Keizer addresses central questions for carers: What does it mean to help? When does help actually hinder? When are we deluding ourselves as we try to help others?

7

Pastoral Carers Consider the Web of Relationships

PASTORAL CARE in our time is as much about facilitating connections as meeting individual needs. Pastoral care for an individual must always include consideration of that individual in their family, extended family, and wider community.

One of the privileges of living in New Zealand from 2007 to 2017 was growing in understanding that individuals are embedded in nuclear families, extended families, and wider communities. Perhaps if I'd been in the United States for that same decade, I might have learned the same lesson, because in that decade, many voices in books, magazines, and other media challenged the individualism of ✱ Western culture.

I saw a concern for extended families and communities in New Zealand expressed in several ways. By strong cultural tradition, everyone is entitled to have a companion with them in stressful *wow!* places like job interviews and medical and legal settings. This convention comes from the influence of Māori, the indigenous people, and from the large number of migrants from the Pacific Islands. Both Māori and Pacific Islanders operate from a profoundly communal perspective, and together they make up almost one-quarter of the New Zealand population.[1]

Two of my friends are ministers of congregations with a significant percentage of Pacific people. My friends have told me so many stories about the ways Pacific Islanders function communally.

> We have to find ways of "entering creatively" into the passion and pathos not only of individuals and small groups but also of whole communities, structures and systems. Persons are deeply affected by the inter-relationships they develop within the communities they participate in. Persons are thus affected for good and ill, by the state of health or disease of the communities they are a part of.
>
> —Emmanuel Y. Lartey, "Global Views for Pastoral Care and Counseling"[2]

Individuals seldom sign up for tasks alone. Instead, they bring their family members along. When an individual serves on a committee or church board, they view themselves as representing their family and community.

Even given the individualism of some cultures, funerals have always been instances where even Western pastoral carers consider families and contexts, including the workplace, clubs, or boards. Often people from various settings in the deceased person's life are invited to say something at the funeral or memorial service. In most Western settings, however, the events involving people from the extended family and wider community that follow a death last only one day.

Sad!

In contrast, one of my friends told me that for the Cook Islanders in her congregation, the mourning process after a death involves morning and evening devotions in the family home every day between the death and the funeral, and the minister is expected to lead the evening devotions. This takes a lot of time, which was disconcerting to my friend at first, but she now appreciates the way relationships in the extended family are nurtured by those devotional times.

In addition, she has grown to appreciate the Cook Islands' ceremony one year after the death of a family member, when the gravestone is unveiled. This marker of the passage of mourning time is something she wishes Westerners would adopt. Māori people in New Zealand also have a ceremony at the one-year mark when the gravestone is unveiled, and Jewish people around the world mark the one-year

Wonderful concept!

anniversary of a family member's death with special observances. This one-year celebration gives family members and friends the opportunity to grieve together one more time, and also to lay down ✓ a portion of their grief because a full year has passed.

Western Christians do a pretty good job with funerals, but do we remember the mourning spouse, children, and extended family over the first year or two after the death? Do we see mourning as a communal practice, or do we expect grieving people to process everything on their own?

Remembering the Many Partners of Care

Peggy Way uses the phrase "the many partners of care"[3] to describe the fact that people who receive pastoral care in congregations have often received, or are still receiving, many other kinds of care as well. She cites the example of an elderly person in a congregation who dies. That person may have received attention from a spouse, family members, a minister, many different members of the congregation, doctors, nurses, hospice workers, chaplains, nursing home staff, insurance representatives, and Social Security staff.

Impt

Way writes, "For this particular situation where prayers have been offered, the caring processes are thick and deep and the partners of care are diverse and crucial for both good dyings and hopeful livings."[4] Way notes that when pastoral care is primarily understood as operating within psychological and counseling paradigms, much of this "thickness and depth" is invisible.

How? Ideas

In the past, pastoral care—apart from funerals and weddings— often focused on individuals. With this growing awareness of the significance of nuclear families, extended families, and wider communities, pastoral carers will profit from taking some time to ponder the primary tasks of pastoral care—healing, sustaining, guiding, reconciling, nurturing, liberating, and empowering—in the light of the web of relationships surrounding care recipients as well as caregivers.

> Ascribe to the Lord, O
>   families of the peoples,
> ascribe to the Lord glory and
>   strength.
>
> —Psalm 96:7

Pastoral care tasks must be performed with the awareness of the way those actions are influenced by the "many partners of care." Sometimes pastoral care consists of helping an individual or family making connections with a partner of care.

In addition to nuclear and extended families, people live in neighborhoods, cities, and countries, and on a globe that is increasingly interconnected. In this chapter, I will look at some ministries that illustrate the way pastoral care in our time takes a wide perspective and considers needs beyond the individual. I will conclude the chapter with a glance at the age-related cohorts that impact pastoral care.

Neighborhood Patterns

In our time in New Zealand, my husband and I lived in a long, narrow valley—appropriately called Northeast Valley—extending northeast from our town, Dunedin. Soon after we moved there, we learned that our local Baptist church had done a demographic study showing that lots of lower-income families lived in very old houses in the valley. At the same time, the New Zealand government began to offer subsidies on insulation for older houses.

The leaders of the Baptist church gathered together a coalition of people from other Northeast Valley churches and community organizations. Together they offered to help families in the valley obtain government money for insulation. They worked with contractors to get the insulation installed. Over the years of the project, many members of churches in the valley built relationships with families living close by.

A few years after the insulation project, a community garden was developed, as well as a community art project. A monthly neighborhood newsletter describes opportunities such as communal jam making and bicycle repair. I believe the insulation project contributed to a neighborhood feel in the valley, which then spilled into other projects. A feeling of community trust, safety, and support

Pastoral care tasks must be performed with the awareness of the way those actions are influenced by the "many partners of care."

contributes to the well-being of everyone, a concern of pastoral caregiving.

Reflecting on the changes I saw in the valley, I'll repeat the question I asked in chapter 1 when I was discussing community gardens: Was the insulation project local mission or was it pastoral care? The answer must be "both." I'll ask a second question: Was the insulation project a way of working for social justice or was it pastoral care? Again, the answer must be "both."

[handwritten margin note: P.C. as a way to do cross-over ministries — great]

People belong to many networks; pastoral care itself is part of a web of ways people care for one another. An illustration on a citywide scale comes from Portland, Oregon, where more than two hundred partnerships have been formed between churches and schools. One of them was formed between a large suburban church and an inner-city high school. The relationship includes food, clothing, mentoring, sports, and beautification programs.[6]

An article in *Christianity Today* explains that the church-school partnerships are only one example of many ways Christian congregations have engaged with the city.

The author of the article, Tony Kriz, an Oregonian, writes and teaches about Christian discipleship in a post-Christian age.

Kriz explains that Portland is one of the first post-Christian cities in the United States, which he defines as a city where less than half of the population is Christian. Working from a minority position gives congregations a lot of opportunities, because minorities are

On the one hand, we are called to play the Good Samaritan on life's roadside, but that will be only an initial act. One day we must come to see that the whole Jericho road must be transformed so that men and women will not be constantly beaten and robbed as they make their journey on life's highway. True compassion is more than flinging a coin to a beggar; it is not haphazard and superficial. It comes to see that an edifice which produces beggars needs restructuring.

—Martin Luther King Jr., "A Time to Break the Silence"[5]

nonthreatening. Often majority groups are perceived as bullies or too powerful, which creates anxiety.

Kriz notes that because Christians in Portland are a minority group, city leaders don't have much anxiety about separation of church and state issues when Christian churches engage with their city. This lack of anxiety, Kris believes, is impacting both the churches in Portland and the city government. He continues:

> The church here can no longer define the terms of engagement, she can no longer claim to have it "figured out," and she is realizing she might just need help from some new friends. The government has realized that the church is not a threat (even in a city as liberal as Portland) and so there is significantly less risk in partnering to solve our shared concerns, even if that help comes from Christians.[7]

Kriz doesn't say whether the churches call their engagement with the city "local mission," "working for social justice," or "pastoral care." Whatever the name, pastoral care is clearly visible within these ministries. Christians don't separate those three forms of ministry as sharply as they used to.

How wonderful that Christians are caring in so many different ways in neighborhoods and cities. These ministries illustrate the web of relationships that all people live within and that pastoral carers must keep in mind.

Other Interconnected Ministries

An additional example of the interconnectedness of pastoral care, local mission, and work for social justice comes from ministry to refugees. Back in the 1980s, our Seattle congregation hosted numerous Hmong refugees from Vietnam, helping them find land for vegetable gardens and helping them market their produce. Later, members of the congregation worked with refugees from several other countries, and one of my friends in the congregation is currently hosting a refugee from Cameroon. Several congregation members, who earlier hosted refugees, have gotten involved in

He has told you, O Mortal, what is good; and what does the Lord require of you but to do justice, and to love kindness, and to walk humbly with your God?

—Micah 6:8

Interconnected pastoral care social justice mission

advocacy for refugees at the Immigration and Naturalization Service Detention Center in Tacoma, Washington.

We have traditionally viewed working for social justice as quite separate from pastoral care, but we now understand that much work for social justice finds its grounding in pastoral care. Care for individuals and groups and advocacy for those groups inform each other.

In addition to refugee ministry, Christians engage in many other forms of care for the marginalized in which hands-on care and advocacy for social justice are closely linked. Many of the prison chaplains I have met are working for prison reform. Everything from domestic violence to youth truancy often has a hands-on component as well as policy implications that advocates focus on.

Caring for the earth illustrates the connections between social justice and pastoral care in a slightly different way. In recent decades, more congregations have been getting involved in ministries called "creation care" or "stewardship of the environment." Many motivations lie behind such ministry.

One motivation comes from the impact of environmental damage on the poor, who are always disproportionately affected by environmental degradation. Consider the example of a toxic waste dump near a neighborhood. When residents become aware of the toxicity of their environment, the more affluent among them are able to move away more quickly and easily. The least affluent usually have fewer options and have to stay there, suffering ongoing damage. Of course, people with the highest incomes would never have

---

Pastoral care has a systemic and social orientation. Although pastoral care is not the same as social change, it is informed—as surely as any other aspect of the church's ministry—by an awareness of the need for social ethical action in specific situations.

—Howard Stone, *Theological Context for Pastoral Caregiving: Word in Deed*[8]

bought a home in that neighborhood or would have pulled strings so the dump would be located elsewhere.

The ongoing effects of climate change further illustrate this phenomenon. Scientists predict that climate change will raise sea levels. Richer countries with land below sea level, such as the Netherlands, will be able to afford to create or raise dikes to hold back the water as sea levels rise.

Bangladesh has been identified by the United Nations as the country most vulnerable to damage from rising seas. A sea level rise of 1.5 meters will affect 16 percent of the land area and 15 percent of the population of Bangladesh, seventeen million people.[9] Working for policies to mitigate climate change will have an impact on an enormous number of people's well-being.

How can advocacy for something happening on the other side of the world be considered to be related to pastoral care? Isn't pastoral care personal and intimate, involving close-up relational connections? In this globalized world, Bangladesh isn't really so far away. Almost everyone has worn clothes manufactured in Bangladesh, met a migrant from there, or known someone who has visited there.

Besides, the very policies that would help reduce sea-level rise in Bangladesh will also benefit people who live right next door—and each of us. Global climate change is beginning to affect daily life in many settings through increasingly erratic and even violent weather, if nothing else.

Concern for global environmental issues may motivate some Christians to engage in local expressions of care for the

Some people use the word _glocal_ to reflect the growing reality that most issues have local and global components. The popular saying "think globally, act locally" reflects the same connection. In a global world, pastoral carers might find themselves engaged in actions with impacts far and wide that never would have been considered to be pastoral care a generation ago.

environment. Local projects such as stream clean up or park rehabilitation create bridges between congregations and their local communities. These projects show that all people live in contexts that include the physical world.

Life Stages

Not only are we individuals embedded in families and other communities, we also travel in cohorts through life. All people born around the same time are influenced by the events that happened throughout their lives, especially in childhood, adolescence, and the teen years. My parents were deeply shaped by the Depression and World War II. My parents' movements through their lifespans were characterized by the frugality, hard work, and stoicism that was necessary during the Depression and World War II, similar to many in their age cohort.

In the same way that people vary in their sense of connection to their nuclear family, extended family, and the community where they live, people vary in their sense of connection to their age cohort. Recently my sons were talking about this. My older son said he identifies pretty strongly with Generation X. He listed several characteristics typical of Gen X that he'd read in an online article, and he talked about the way he saw those characteristics in himself. My younger son, who was born in 1982, close to the transition between Gen X and the millennials, said he does not identify very much with either Gen X or the millennials.

* Learning about generational and life-stage patterns can be helpful in pastoral care. Like my younger son, not all individuals fit into the commonly described generational patterns, so pastoral carers should learn about generational and life-stage patterns, but hold them lightly, especially because experts disagree on the exact birth dates when each generation begins and ends.

I wrote two books about midlife, which I defined as thirty-five to fifty-five. Some writers extend midlife to sixty. Because of the interviews I conducted and the patterns the interviews revealed, when I talk with someone between thirty-five and sixty, I am not surprised if they have questions about faith that are making them feel off balance, or if they are finding new pleasure in silence, mystery, and reflection as components of faith. I'm not surprised if they talk about challenges that come from feeling sandwiched between the needs of their children and the needs of their parents.

If I talk with people in that age bracket who have never been married or who have never had children, I expect that they might be processing a sense of loss. Not all people at midlife fit the patterns I heard about in my interviews, but knowing the patterns helps me know the kinds of questions to ask, while being open to a variety of answers.

In the same way, if I talk to a baby boomer, I am not surprised if they were influenced by the Vietnam War and Watergate. Knowing the patterns helps us listen more deeply.

One of the conundrums about age and stage in pastoral care is the lack of clear language to differentiate between seniors who are in very different places. One of my friends, who just turned sixty-five, finds it odd that she and her ninety-year-old father are both considered "seniors," even though she is working full-time and takes

Pastoral care needs may vary depending on the age cohort of care recipients. The generations in our society, with their own distinct characteristics, are often described like this:

- Gen Z, iGen, or Centennials: Born 2005 and later
- Millennials or Gen Y: Born 1982 to 2004
- Gen X: Born 1965 to 1981
- Baby Boomers: Born 1946 to 1964
- Traditionalists or Silent Generation: Born 1945 and before

long wilderness canoe trips as vacation, while he has been fully retired for several decades, and his health is frail.

One study from twenty-five years ago proposed this language: the young old (sixty to sixty-nine), the middle old (seventy to seventy-nine), and the very old (eighty-plus).[10] However, soon after that proposal, shortcomings in that language became clear. The pastoral care needs of a sixty-eight-year-old who is working and another sixty-eight-year-old with a chronic disease are also very different, even though they are both "young old." However, those two sixty-eight-year-olds will have some common memories, experiences, and influences because of their age.

Patterns based on age and generation matter for pastoral carers, but they are not the only factors to consider when meeting an individual. People are shaped by their age cohort, life stage, nuclear families, extended families, and wider communities, as well as their unique genetic inheritance, innate gifts, and personality traits.

The Living Human Web

Because of the variety of contexts in which people live, Pamela Cooper-White, Anglican priest, psychotherapist, and seminary professor, talks about the need for "a web of resources gathered collaboratively to address the complex, layered needs and struggles"[11] of care receivers. She believes that an important tool for carers is a collection of email addresses and cell phone entries representing "a wide variety of *personally known and trusted* helpers in the community with various expertise, including spiritual directors, social workers, school officials and educators, medical professionals, public agency workers, and community organizers."[12]

Cooper-White describes a pattern of pastoral care in our time that echoes several of the themes in the opening chapters of this book. Offering care in our time, she emphasizes,

> Patterns based on age and generation matter for pastoral carers, but they are not the only factors to consider when meeting an individual.

Yes— needed Early collection in new locale

Wimberly case studies ↖

Training Tips

If you lead training sessions for pastoral carers, be sure to

1 Present models that show the significance of families and extended families in giving and receiving pastoral care.

2 Discuss examples of ministries that integrate pastoral care, social justice, and local mission.

3 Discuss the significance of age cohorts and life stages in pastoral care settings.

4 Share local resources with each other, including spiritual directors, social workers, school officials and educators, medical professionals, public agency workers, and community organizers.

means sharing the responsibility and authority for pastoral care with trained and empowered lay caregivers, such as Lay Eucharistic Ministers, small-group leaders, Stephen Ministers, parish nurses, and pastoral care teams. It means hitting the pavements to identify and join with others who are working in the community to change the conditions that perpetuate suffering, and bringing those individuals back into our congregations as witnesses to the wider needs of the community. It also means seeking consultation.[13]

The four skills discussed in part 2 of this book will help pastoral carers recognize the networks that surround each person receiving and offering pastoral care:

• Stress is often related to relational and physical contexts.
• Listening skills help carers understand the web of relationships surrounding care recipients.
• Spiritual practices help carers live in a receptive stance, enabling insight into care receivers' contexts.
• Habits that promote resilience help carers thrive in all the settings and relationships of their own lives.

For Reflection and Discussion

1 What have you observed from people from other cultures or ethnicities about how they perceive the significance of nuclear and extended families? What would you like to learn from what you have observed?

2 Have you seen examples of pastoral care overlapping with local mission or social-justice efforts? In what ways have you seen these examples contribute to healing, sustaining, guiding, reconciling, nurturing, liberating, and empowering?

3 What life-stage patterns do you think are particularly significant for pastoral care? What do you think are the limits of focusing on age cohorts and life stages?

4 Think about the web of relationships in your own life. Which relationships have had the most impact on you—nuclear family, extended family, people at church, workmates, friends, members of clubs or other organizations? What has been the nature of that impact on your engagement with pastoral care? Write a prayer for yourself as a pastoral carer who is embedded in a web of relationships.

Resources

Graham, Elaine L. *Transforming Practice: Pastoral Theology in an Age of Uncertainty*. Eugene, OR: Wipf & Stock, 2002.

> Explores Christian ministry and pastoral care in a fragmented, relativistic, and pluralistic world and provides a framework for reflection on pastoral care in our time.

Doehring, Carrie. *The Practice of Pastoral Care: A Postmodern Approach.* Louisville: Westminster John Knox, 2015. ck on my shelf

> A fascinating exploration of pastoral care that draws on three patterns: premodern (apprehending God through religious rituals), modern (consulting rational and empirical sources), and postmodern (acknowledging the contextual nature of knowledge).

Part Two

Skills for Pastoral Care

8

Old/New Sources of Stress

WHEN I was a young adult, I came across an article in our local Seattle newspaper about a stress scale. Each major life event was assigned a number of points. The article said that the higher the cumulative points, the more likely that a person would get sick.

I was fascinated by the list of forty-three events. The scale assigned points up to one hundred for each event. Things like changes in sleep habits or recreation earned points in the teens. Moving to a new place and trouble with a boss earned points in the twenties. Also in the twenties was an outstanding personal achievement. Hmm, I found myself thinking, is it true that positive events can be stressful? Yes, the research indicated that both positive and negative events cause stress.

I had recently gotten married. I was thrilled about marrying a man I loved. However, in the weeks before the wedding, I experienced a great deal of stress, ate too many cookies for comfort, and gained about ten pounds in a couple of months. My mother, who had sewn my wedding dress for me, was worried that I wouldn't fit into it. When I read the stress scale, I was pleased to see that getting married was ranked at fifty points. No wonder I experienced a disconcerting amount of stress before such a positive event.

Only six events garnered more points than getting married: personal injury or illness (fifty-three), death of a close family member (sixty-three), a jail term (sixty-three), marital separation (sixty-

> Stress can be defined as feeling overwhelmed and/or unable to cope effectively with people or events in one's life.
>
> —Barbara J. Carlozzi et al., "Spirituality, Anger, and Stress in Early Adolescents"[1]
>
> Stress is a condition where the demands of one's environment exceed one's resources.
>
> —Pauline Boss, *Family Stress Management*[2]

five), divorce (seventy-three), and death of a spouse at one hundred points.

Many years later, I learned that the research for the list of points for stressful events, called the Social Readjustment Rating Scale,[3] was conducted at the University of Washington in Seattle, explaining why I read about it in my local paper. Many more years passed before I understood that the list has severe limitations, including the fact that it doesn't take into account coping strategies or individual circumstances.

For example, maybe one or both of the parties in a divorce feel a great sense of relief that the marriage is coming to an end. In that instance, the intensity of the stress might be significantly less.

Despite its limitations, the scale remains helpful for carers, as long as two other major ways of viewing stress are held in tension with it. In this chapter, I'll highlight three ways to view stress that have come out of research. I'll explain the relevance of the three views for pastoral carers.

Three Perspectives on Stress

Alongside inventories measuring stress, such as the Social Readjustment Rating Scale and a scale often used alongside it, the Hassles Scale, a great deal of research has been conducted on the physiological components of stress. A third way of looking at stress includes a focus on coping strategies as well as stressors, a more holistic approach that is also valuable for carers.

Physiological Components of Stress

An astonishing array of hormones floods the body when we experience stress. Scientists tell us that these hormones play a significant role in the fight-or-flight pattern that kept our ancestors safe from wild animals and natural disasters.

We no longer face tigers or grizzly bears on a daily basis, but our bodies still have the ability to mobilize us for rapid response. Every time our bodies prepare to leap into action, stress hormones like cortisol and adrenaline surge into our bloodstream. This flood of stress hormones is helpful in giving us energy and alertness to face challenges, but we also pay a price physiologically.

Several decades ago, stress was viewed as primarily cognitive and emotional. Now we know coping with stress involves the whole body.

Overeating is my knee-jerk response to stress, but in recent years I have come a long way in eating well and keeping my weight at a healthy level. Two years ago, I experienced an extremely stressful year because my husband was ill, I was dealing with complications from a knee replacement that did not heal properly, I was travelling a lot to do public speaking, and we were preparing for a major move. I found myself gaining one or two pounds every month.

mindset
mindtools.com
Holmes + Rahe
scale

For several days—or even up to several weeks—after encountering trauma, people tend to experience a number of effects. Some of them are physical, some are cognitive, some are emotional, some are behavioral, and some are spiritual. But almost all of these effects emanate from the neurochemical and even physiological changes that take place in the brain as a result of experiencing or being exposed to trauma.

—Jeanne L. Jensma, "Critical Incident Intervention with Missionaries"[4]

I couldn't figure out what was happening. I was exercising the same amount as I had done for many years. I wasn't overeating by any measure I had ever used before. I wasn't engaging in the binge-eating patterns that had been common in my earlier life, which had caused my mother to worry about whether or not my wedding dress would fit.

Finally, I recognized that the stress hormones my body was releasing were changing my physiology.[5] The most important thing I could do for my weight, I decided, was to work on coping with the stress better.

I took action to change the things I had control over. I said no to all new invitations to travel and speak. I tried to stretch out all the activities and tasks around moving as much as I could, tackling them slowly over many months. I went to counseling to learn how to think more productively about my husband's illness and my irritating knee.

Over the next few months, I could feel the stress lightening. The weight gain slowed, then stopped. I felt so relieved.

Carers can expect that care recipients who are under stress or who have experienced trauma will experience physiological repercussions from the challenging life events they are facing. Some people gain or lose weight. Some develop insomnia and others sleep more. Digestive issues are common, which is easy to understand because many of us get an uneasy feeling in our stomach when facing challenges.

Stress appears to impact almost every system in the body. Stress hormones influence the management of diabetes.[6] I certainly experienced a change in the way I metabolized food when too many stress hormones were present for too long. Even joint problems can be connected to stress. Stress hormones stimulate inflammation in the body, which has far-reaching effects on joints, heart health, and other organ systems.

Stress appears to impact almost every system in the body.

Many doctors, psychologists, and researchers are concerned that too many people are living with levels of chronic stress that are damaging our bodies. The number of people experiencing big events like divorce or the death of a spouse may not be higher than in the past, but everyday stressors add up.

Raymond Yung, a professor in the Department of Internal Medicine at the University of Michigan, focuses his research on immune and inflammatory diseases. He says, "Acute stress is when we got chased by a saber-toothed tiger. Chronic stress is a bad marriage or work anxiety, which we know has an effect on inflammation as well."[7]

A physiological view of stress makes clear the importance of referral to a variety of health-care professionals. Providing help with exercising, eating well, and sleep strategies—or referring care recipients for help in those areas—may not seem to be typical pastoral care actions. However, the physiological components of stress may make that kind of help essential.

A friend of mine, Barbara, is a marriage and family counselor. I asked her what she would recommend to pastoral caregivers who want to help people deal with stress, and she said that when stressed, "Your system doesn't just slow down when you want it to. Each person has to learn how to slow down their body. One simple way is to pay attention to your breathing, trying to slightly lengthen the exhale."

She went on to talk about the significance of Christian contemplative prayer and meditation. She expressed frustration that when most people, including Christians, think about meditation, the first thing that comes to mind is Eastern religions. Yet Christianity, she said, has a "long and strong tradition of contemplation and meditation." Recovering that tradition would help with the physiological aspects of stress, she believes. Her observations highlight the significance of Christian spiritual practices, which will be explored in chapter 10.

> Happy are those
> who do not follow the advice of the wicked,
> or take the path that sinners tread,
> or sit in the seat of scoffers;
> but their delight is in the law of the Lord,
> and on his law they meditate day and night.
> They are like trees
> planted by streams of water,
> which yield their fruit in its season,
> and their leaves do not wither.
> In all that they do, they prosper.
>
> —Psalm 1:1–3

Physiological responses to stress vary with the intensity of the stress. That's why stress inventories are important to know about, even if they are not the only way to view stress.

Scales that Measure Stress (event-oriented)

In the 1960s, Thomas Holmes and Richard Rahe conducted research about the relative stress of forty-three various major life events. In 1967, they published the Social Readjustment Rating Scale, described above. Their research indicated that when people amass more than three hundred points on the scale over a twelve-month period, they have an 80 percent chance of developing a stress-related illness, illustrating that stress is cumulative.[8]

For most people, the major life events on the Holmes and Rahe Scale don't happen all that frequently. In the following decade, researchers began to explore other sources of stress that could be measured. Allen Kanner and a group of researchers published a Hassles Scale in 1981 with 117 specific descriptions of stressful daily events such as losing things, rising prices, home maintenance challenges, concerns about weight, and crime. Their research found that the accumulation of these daily hassles contributes to stress-related outcomes such as anxiety and depression more frequently than major life events.[9]

Pastoral carers need to know that patterns of stress have been measured by researchers. The death of a spouse or close family member is usually shattering, as is divorce and incarceration in most cases. Carers need to know that daily challenges also create stress. The scales I've mentioned here, and others, reveal patterns that can help carers draw people out and listen carefully when care recipients are experiencing stressors that have been shown to be difficult for most people.

Carers also need to know about the limitations of scales like *Yes* these. The scales simply do not measure individual differences between people, including variations in personality, convictions, and responses. My friend Barbara, marriage and family counselor, provides a vivid example of the way differences between people influence stress. Barbara says she has worked with many widows and widowers whose spouses suffered from dementia. One of them will say to Barbara, "Why am I grieving? The dementia was so hard to deal with that I longed for her to have the relief of death, but I am still so sad. I feel overwhelmed."

The next person says, "I grieved before he died, and I am frankly so relieved he's not suffering anymore. I've been surprised at how little grief I'm experiencing after his death. It's simply a giant relief. I feel a sense of freedom."

In general, Americans recognize that their stress levels remain high and exceed what they consider to be healthy. Adults seem to understand the importance of healthy behaviors like managing their stress levels, eating right, getting enough sleep and exercise, but they report experiencing challenges practicing these healthy behaviors. They report being too busy as a primary barrier preventing them from better managing their stress, and a lack of motivation, energy and time as the chief reasons for not being more physically active.

—American Psychological Association, "Stress in America Findings"[10]

Almost all of the stressors listed on the various stress scales still exist. Psychologists have continued to update stress scales since the first scale in the 1960s,[11] and these newer scales still reflect the significance of "old" sources of stress such as death, job loss, financial pressures, and various forms of abuse. These stressors continue to have an impact on caregivers and care recipients.

However, because even the most recent scales are based on research conducted over several years or even decades, they don't include many of the new stressors that are common today, including political polarization; pressure to measure up on social media; expectations from employers, friends, and family members to be connected all the time; changes in employment caused by automation, online shopping, and phone apps like Uber; and other rapidly changing societal patterns.

When my younger son was in his twenties, he often talked about the pressure many of his friends felt to not take all the vacation from work that was allotted to them. Their employers communicated directly or indirectly that a loyal employee would be available to work all the time. This stressor would have been almost unimaginable a few decades ago, but it was very real among his friends. Confirming this experience, a 2015 article in *The Guardian* notes that 41 percent of Americans don't take all the vacation days allotted to them.[12]

Another stressor that certainly existed a few decades ago but influences more people today comes from migration and the resulting stress of dislocation or unsettledness. In countries where the majority of people speak English as their first language, the percentage of people who were not born in the country where they live ranges from 12 percent in the United Kingdom to 27 percent in Australia. In the United States, 13 percent of residents were not born in this country.[13] These figures have increased a great deal in recent decades.

When pastoral carers talk to migrants or their children—even if those children were born in the new country—they can expect to hear about a number of stressors that come from living with a sense of dislocation. This applies to the well-paid engineer who was born abroad, as well as to refugees who experience an even greater degree of dislocation because of the trauma that preceded their arrival here.

Pastoral carers today need to pay attention to the stressors that are common in their context. Different communities will have varying patterns of major and everyday stressors. Carers need to know about the pattern of stress in their community as well as the coping strategies that are commonly used.

③ Stress, Coping Strategies, and Meaning

Individuals differ in their response to stress because of variations in personality, past experiences, coping strategies, and the ways they think about events. One of the earliest research studies of stress in families was conducted in the 1940s. Sociologist Reuben Hill looked at families in which the father was absent during World War 2. Hill came up with the ABC-X model for stress, which takes into account differences between people. Hill's model has been adapted by many researchers in recent years. The components of the later models remain similar to the factors Hill observed during and after the war.

The components of stress, Hill argues, are:

- An event (A)
- The family's crisis-meeting resources (B)
- The meaning the family gives to the event (C)

These three factors working together produce a crisis response (X).[15] Hill's ABC-X model and the later models grounded in his work are more holistic than simply assigning points to various stressors because these models take into account the response of individuals and families.

One of the more recent models, Family Adjustment and Adaptation Response (FAAR), uses this vocabulary:

- Demands (stressors, strains, daily hassles)
- Capabilities (resources and coping behaviors)
- Meanings (situational family identity and worldview)[16]

The vocabulary used in these models will be helpful to pastoral carers, who can use the words or ideas in these models as they ask questions. "Tell me about the resources you feel you have as you face this situation." "How does this situation change the way you view yourselves as a family?"

The models point out the synergy between the demands we experience and the ways we respond to those demands. The presence in our lives of demands and stressors does not necessarily mean those events or relationships will be debilitating, because most people have ways of acting and thinking that help them deal with the stress, at least to some extent.

Coping strategies do make a difference in the ways people respond to stress. Physical exercise, time with friends, finding pleasure in art or music, prayer, meditation, taking naps, reading favorite novels, or watching well-loved TV series or movies—all of these and other ways to find relief from stress help a lot. Pastoral carers can help care recipients brainstorm how to further develop coping strategies.

Positive Responses / Note the negative also

Equally influential is the way the event is framed. "This is really hard, but I know the outcome will be worth it" contrasts greatly with "this pain will never end, and nothing good can possibly come from it." One of the significant roles in pastoral care is to help care recipients explore various ways to frame the events they are experiencing.

Framing : Re-framing

One major resource mentioned in much of the literature on stress is social support, which can include relationships with family and friends, various kinds of small groups, and relationships in the workplace or neighborhood. In chapter 2, I told you about my husband's very positive experience as a member of a pastoral care team and his frustration at another church with the pastoral care role he took on. One of the significant differences was the lack of social support at the second church.

The pastoral care team at the first church met monthly for training and brainstorming about the pastoral care needs in the congregation. They prayed at length for the people receiving care. They worked together, chatting all the while, as they cooked meals that they would place in the church freezer and later deliver to families. The social support Dave received as a member of the pastoral care team enabled him to deal with the challenges of providing pastoral care to people in need who were sometimes not easy to deal with.

The time with the other pastoral carers also helped Dave assign meaning to the hard parts of giving pastoral care. The pastoral care team talked together about why they were engaging in caring, even when that care was very challenging.

Ironically, all too frequently the social settings of our lives create stress, rather than providing social support. Pastoral carers need to ask about the web of relationships that surround care recipients, acknowledging that not all relationships are supportive.

My friend Michele, a psychiatric nurse practitioner, gives an example of dealing with stress that encompasses both coping strategies and meaning making. Michele has provided training a couple of times for parents of autistic children. Michele believes parents of all children, but especially those with special needs, need to think very carefully about where their own personhood ends and where the child's personhood begins—in other words, the boundary between the parent's and child's ownership of a situation.

An autistic child might say, "You made me hit you." Michele notes that the parent needs to respond, "I did not make you hit me. You chose to hit me." Underlying these words, parents need to nurture an attitude of "This is your problem, not mine. I am willing to walk beside you, but I am not willing to own your problems."

Informal social support networks are important for health and well-being and can be particularly helpful in difficult times. Social interactions involving support network members, however, can also be a source of stress.

—Karen D. Lincoln et al., "Social Support, Traumatic Events, and Depressive Symptoms Among African Americans"[17]

Michele argues that when anyone assumes ownership of problems that actually belong to another person, bitterness is likely to result. She cites Hebrews 12:15: "See to it that no one fails to obtain the grace of God; that no root of bitterness springs up and causes trouble." She has observed that bitterness rooted in inadequate boundaries causes significant trouble for the parent, the child, and others in the family system.

Michele believes that one of the biggest challenges in pastoral caregiving is very needy people who can "suck you dry." She emphasizes the significance of teamwork in pastoral care, so team members can help each other cope with very needy people. A sense of clear ownership of problems can also help in conversations with people whose needs never seem to end.

Because caregivers usually have soft hearts and want to care, determining and articulating clear ownership of problems is often difficult but fruitful. As caregivers, we need clarity about who problems belong to, while we are encouraging care recipients—whether they are parents of autistic children or people with other challenging relationships—to learn how to articulate the ownership of stressors in their own lives as well.

Exploring ownership issues is a coping strategy, because it helps us deal with stressors in a healthier way. We assign a different meaning to the stressors we're experiencing when we believe a problem is ours to solve, compared with situations in which we know we are accompanying people who are dealing with problems that belong to them.

This third, more holistic way of looking at stress, focused on the relationship between stress, coping strategies, and meanings, will help pastoral carers steer conversations—by asking good questions and using reflecting—in the areas of demands, resources, and ways of framing events. The questions and reflecting must be gentle, because the danger of putting too much emphasis on this model is that stressed people can feel it is their fault they are not coping better with the stress.

Because caregivers usually have soft hearts and want to care, determining and articulating clear ownership of problems is often difficult but fruitful.

Consider this question: "Why is it so hard for you accept that the ownership of this problem actually rests with your sister?" A question like that can sound like the carer blames the care recipient for not coping better. A question like, "What forms of exercise do you engage in to relieve stress?" can make care recipients feel that they are falling short in more than one way. They're not coping with the stressful situation and also failing to take good care of themselves.

Carers need to help stressed people explore resources and coping strategies without implying that better use of the resources and ways of coping will completely remove the effects of the stress or lessen the stress dramatically. Caregivers need to help stressed people think about the meaning they assign to the stressful situation, without implying that positive thinking will bring complete relief from stress.

The holistic model of stress emphasizes the synergy between stressors and the way people deal with them. The biological model of stress helps us understand that stressors create changes to our physiology, no matter how well we're coping. The stress inventories help us remember that major stressors have predictable impacts on most people. These three models must be held together in order to help stressed people wisely.

Reframing Stress

The book *Sacred Stress* presents a Christian perspective on coping with stress that builds on all three models. One of the authors, Heather Wright, directs a counseling center, and in the book she draws on what she has learned from counseling clients about healthy ways to cope with stress. She also tells the story of her own experience of severe stress at the time of her divorce.

Wright and her former husband were not only marriage partners but also coworkers, so the divorce had implications both in her home and at work. In addition, part of the stress of the divorce

> The holistic model of stress emphasizes the synergy between stressors and the way people deal with them.

came from the shame that she couldn't fix her marriage, despite her expertise as a counselor in what makes marriages work.

When her marriage was falling apart, someone told Wright that stress is cumulative. She reflects:

> At the time, the thought that "stress is cumulative" helped me make sense of it all. But while there may be some wisdom in that phrase, there is also a negativity and fatalism to it as well. As a result, I thought life must be about trying to avoid stress and thereby avoid the outcome that would be produced by too much stress. I became afraid and avoided stress. I now realize that stress does not have to be cumulative nor is it a death sentence for a marriage.[18]

Wright and her coauthor on *Sacred Stress*, George R. Faller, argue that stress can motivate us to grow in very important areas of life. Faller was a firefighter in Manhattan on September 11, 2001, and his life was changed by the trauma he experienced that day and in the following months as he helped fellow firefighters deal with the experience. He grew in his ability to be vulnerable with loved ones and to rely on them in new ways.

Faller reflects, "I began to discover the treasure buried alongside the hurt. Stress isn't my enemy; it is my companion. Stress sets the stage for turning separateness into wholeness. Experiencing the benefits of facing stress with another person propelled me to help others do the same."[20]

Positive religious coping is characterized as an adaptive coping strategy that includes: (a) religious forgiveness, (b) seeking spiritual support, (c) reframing of stressful event to view it as a potentially beneficial opportunity for growth and learning, and (d) finding meaning in a negative situation through spiritual connectedness with a higher power.

—Mariana Sanchez et al., "The Impact of Religious Coping on the Acculturative Stress and Alcohol Use of Recent Latino Immigrants"[19]

Wright and Faller describe the ways their faith developed because of these two major stressful events in their lives. As they processed the stress with others and as they drew near to God with their pain, they grew in trusting God and seeing God as active in their daily lives. They received love from God in new ways.

They argue that ⟨stress can be an opportunity for growth⟩ when we

- reframe stress as an opportunity for growth as well as a challenge to be dealt with;
- allow ourselves to feel the emotions raised by the stressful situation rather than try to suppress them;
- turn toward others with vulnerability and honesty and allow others to care for us; and
- turn toward God with our pain and receive God's love, which comes to us in so many ways.[21]

Faller and Wright use the language of "befriending stress." They advocate accepting the place of stress into our lives: "Stress is essential for healthy living. Like a racehorse in training, stress allows us to stretch our strides farther and increase our galloping speed. Our lives can be so much healthier if we think positively about stress and use the vulnerability it creates to strengthen our relationships."[22]

When we fear stress, when we're adding up stress points with the assumption that being debilitated by major stress is inevitable, we easily become paralyzed in difficult situations. When we affirm that we have learned many coping strategies over our lifespan and that we know we are surrounded by helpful resources, we are able to access our creativity, energy, and gifts.[23]

Our physiological response to stress is influenced by our thoughts. Optimism about our ability to cope helps to reduce the physiological components of the stress response. Focusing on God's love in every circumstance and the gift of God's peace slows our racing hearts.

Our physiological response to stress is influenced by our thoughts.

The psychiatric nurse practitioner I mentioned earlier, Michele, stresses ⟨the importance of thankfulness as a component of stress management.⟩ She believes that a strong emphasis on the importance of optimism can backfire because we can encourage a hyper-positive attitude that is based more on denial than on reality. *Exactly*

Practicing thankfulness, on the other hand, enables us to look at our lives to see the good gifts God has given. In contrast with denial, which is a pattern of putting aside negative things as if they don't ✻ exist, choosing thankfulness shifts our focus to gifts and blessings we can easily miss.

Michele has found that parents of autistic children who can appreciate the uniqueness of their children tend to cope better with the stress of parenting. ⟨Thankfulness—even while acknowledging the challenges—gives meaning.⟩ Practicing gratitude shifts the perspective of the parents in a way that enables them to befriend stress.

Hope and Stress

The additional volumes in this series focus on how to nurture hope in the midst of common stressors today. The volumes address many topics, such as death and loss, unemployment, dementia, addiction, chronic illness, trauma in relationships, children with developmental challenges, and mental health issues. The books give information about the stressors and focus on resources, coping strategies, and meanings as well.

Hope in the midst of stress comes from many sources, and each of the three models for stress presented in this chapter can play a role in nurturing hope. Understanding the transitory nature of the ① physiological response to stress and using practices to help slow our bodies help us hold onto hope. The stress inventories help us ② see patterns of stress and help us know we are not alone; hope can come from feeling solidarity with others who experience the same kinds of situations.

All 3 are valuable

③ The holistic model of stress helps us affirm that drawing on resources and developing coping strategies really does make a positive difference when we experience stress. Choosing to be vulnerable with others about what we're thinking and feeling can help us draw on social support. And hope is nurtured when we reframe stress as an opportunity to grow individually and as a family, and also as an invitation to deeper faith.

These components of hope will help pastoral carers when we experience stress and will also help us when as we desire to serve care recipients.

For Reflection and Discussion

1 Spend some time pondering the three perspectives of stress presented in this chapter. Which one tends to shape your thinking most often? Which one might you benefit from keeping in mind more often? What benefits can you see from holding the three perspectives in tension?

2 What are the biggest stressors in your life? What are your resources and coping strategies? What meanings do you assign to

the stressors? What new coping strategies and meanings would you like to develop?

3 When you listen to care recipients talk about the stressors in their lives, what kinds of questions do you usually ask? What new questions would you like to ask?

4 What might it look like for you to "befriend stress"? Look back on the stressors on your life and ponder the way they have shaped you. Write a prayer for yourself as a carer who desires to grow by facing stress as wisely as possible and who helps others befriend stress.

Resources

Faller, George, and Heather P. Wright. *Sacred Stress: A Radically Different Approach to Using Life's Challenges for Positive Change.* Woodstock, VT: Skylight Paths, 2016.

Faller and Wright advocate for vulnerability in relationships and optimism when facing stress. The book contains many ideas that will be helpful to caregivers for themselves and for times they want to steer care recipients in healthy directions.

Brown, Brené. *Daring Greatly: How the Courage to Be Vulnerable Transforms the Way We Live, Love, Parent, and Lead.* New York: Gotham, 2012.

Because social support is so significant in coping with stress, and because vulnerability is essential in receiving social support, Brown's book provides a foundation for a healthy response to stress.

Rohr, Richard. *Breathing Under Water: Spirituality and the Twelve Steps.* Cincinnati, OH: St. Anthony Messenger Press, 2011.

For people dealing with the stress of addiction and destructive behaviors, the Twelve Steps are usually very helpful. Rohr provides a Christian interpretation of the Twelve Steps as a way to grow in experiencing God's love and compassion.

9

Listening Skills

MY MOTHER remembers an incident when the priest in her parish was heading out of town, and he asked her to take communion to a woman in the hospital who was dying. The patient was quite young, in her thirties, and her husband was there in the hospital room with her. Mom greeted the couple, pulled the door closed, chatted very briefly, and began the communion liturgy. A few moments into the communion service, someone knocked on the door. Mom answered, and it turned out to be a man with a name badge saying "Chaplain."

Mom invited him to join in the communion service. In response to her invitation, he asked what she believed about communion, whether the elements really became Christ's body and blood or whether they were only symbols. Mom did her best to mask her shock at the question. She replied by saying that the patient was quite ill, so this was not the time to discuss that issue. The chaplain declined to come in, and Mom continued with the communion liturgy. The woman died only hours later.

Mom was quite unsettled by this incident and debriefed with her priest after he returned from his trip. He affirmed that Mom had handled the man's totally inappropriate question as well as possible.

Listening Requires Receptivity

In this chapter, I am writing about listening skills for pastoral care, and the story of this strange incident in a hospital room may

For everything there is a season, and a time for every matter under heaven: . . . a time to keep silence, and a time to speak.

—Ecclesiastes 3:1, 7

seem to have little to do with listening. In *Life Together*, German theologian Dietrich Bonhoeffer writes, "Our love for others is learning to listen to them."[1] Love enables us to come into situations with expectancy.

The chaplain my mother encountered, as soon as he heard "communion," engaged with his own theological convictions and priorities about communion, rather than paying attention to the people in that hospital room. His behavior provides a negative illustration for what I view as the background commitment for good listening skills: noticing and being receptive to what's going on in a situation or in a person's life.

Not about me!

Being receptive requires a kind of holy curiosity that enables us to wonder what God is doing in a situation before—and after—we arrive. Being receptive helps us slow down a bit and pay attention to what's already happening in the lives of the people we encounter, their thoughts, feelings, concerns, passions, and desires.

Love motivates us to work on improving our ability to listen. In order to listen well, we have to want to listen. In order to want to listen, we have to expect that something is worth listening to, that something real and significant is happening in the lives of the people we encounter. This expectant stance is what I view as being receptive.

> In pastoral care, we listen for many different reasons, including to get the facts about a situation, to find out how care recipients view their circumstances, to learn how to pray for the person, to offer support, to express empathy and compassion, to allow people to process their thoughts and feelings out loud, and to open up a space where people can talk about the overlap between their daily life and their sense of God or the holy. Unanswered questions are common in many situations of grief and stress, and carers do not need to have the answers to those questions. Listening in itself shows love and reflects the presence and love of God.

> Fortunately, communication scholars all agree that listening skills can be learned.

Fortunately, communication scholars all agree that listening skills can be learned. A little effort goes a long way in helping us listen better. That effort may take the form of learning about the listening skills described in this chapter, consciously trying to use them in new ways, and asking for feedback about how well we are listening. That effort might include practicing the skills in a workshop setting.

I find it helpful to think about five areas of listening skills: *Assign activities*

- Keeping people talking
- Guiding conversations
- Expressing empathy
- Understanding contrasts in listening
- Dealing with inner noise

This chapter is arranged around those five areas, and as I walk through each of them, I will give particular attention to the way the various skills relate to listening in pastoral care. I will also stress the aspects of the listening skills that help to empower care recipients.

Skills that Keep People Talking

My husband has been mentoring a young man who is shattered by a breakup that happened several months ago. Recently I overheard Dave talking to a friend about this relationship. Dave said, "All I do is listen, and after almost every conversation he says, 'Thanks so much. This has been so helpful.' But I don't do anything except listen. Whenever I give him advice, he's really not receptive to it, so I've stopped giving it."

Another reason it might be appropriate in a pastoral care setting to simply encourage the person to keep talking is that sometimes people discover their own inner wisdom and arrive at a solution to their problem on their own. If we want to help people find their own strength, then giving them space to arrive at their own solutions through careful listening is an important strategy.

We encourage people to keep talking, without guiding the conversation, in three ways:

- Body language
- Minimal encouragers
- Silence

Body Language

The position of our body and our facial expressions are a type of language. We communicate with them. Most people have experienced the difference between an attentive listener who is leaning toward us and watching our eyes versus someone who is staring into space or watching a TV screen on the opposite wall and looking bored when we are talking. As you listen, pay attention to the way your body is communicating.

Minimal Encouragers

Most people use small words and phrases, called minimal encouragers, to encourage others to keep talking. These small comments indicate to speakers that we are following what they're saying. As I've studied listening skills, I've found that most people get into a rut with their minimal encouragers and tend to use the same one over and over, which sounds robotic.

I've observed that I tend to pick a minimal encourager and use it for a year or so, then move on to another one. My most recent minimal encourager is "wow," and by paying attention I can see how often I use it. I am working on using a variety rather than just one, so I can avoid sounding mechanical. Even when I'm listening carefully, if I use the same minimal encourager over and over, I will sound mechanical, and it will seem that I'm not listening well.

Silence

Silence on the part of a listener can be a great gift in a conversation. Robert Bolton, a consultant who offers training in communication skills, notes, "Learning the art of silent responsiveness is essential to

Love motivates us to work on improving our ability to listen. In order to listen well, we have to want to listen. In order to want to listen, we have to expect that something is worth listening to, that something real and significant is happening in the lives of the people we encounter.

good idea

Some examples of minimal encouragers:		
Mmm	Uh-huh	Tell me more.
Oh?	For instance?	I see.
Right	Then?	So?
I hear you.	You bet.	Yes
Really?	Gosh	And?
Go on.	Sure	Darn!
Yeah	Wow	Okay[2]

good listening. After all, another person cannot describe a problem if you are doing all the talking."[3]

Being quiet is a big challenge for many people. Bolton observes that most listeners talk too much, sometimes speaking even more than the person they are attempting to listen to. Bolton is adamant that with practice most people can become more comfortable with silence in conversations.

But if silence is so challenging, why is it worth trying to become more comfortable with it? Why is it important to keep people talking?

As Bolton points out, we won't have accurate information about what's going on in people's circumstances, emotions, or spiritual life if we don't let them talk. Accurate information is essential in pastoral care. Bolton lists many additional benefits of silence. Silence allows speakers to think about what they want to say, clarify their thoughts, experience the feelings churning inside, and proceed at their own pace. Silence is a gentle nudge to go deeper.[5]

Silence conveys balm in times of sorrow, pain, and struggle. In times of joy, silence—coupled with a smile—shows that the listener is celebrating alongside the speaker. Silence, coupled with attentive body language, conveys acceptance, care, companionship, and a willingness to let care recipients define and explore the issue for themselves.

Great — *Let the person tell me —*

It is a listening skill to acknowledge the person who is talking.

It is a listening skill to help keep the conversation going.

It is a listening skill to show some approval of the other person and what they are saying.

It is a listening skill to be able to feed back to the other person what they said and intended rather than what you selected from what they said.

—Richard Dimbelby and Graeme Burton, *More Than Words: An Introduction to Communication*[4]

When Bolton trains people in listening skills, more than half of the participants are initially uncomfortable with silence. He notes:

Even a few seconds' pause in a conversation causes many of them to squirm. These people feel so ill at ease with silences that they have a strong inner compulsion to shatter the quiet with questions, advice, or any other sound that will end their discomfort by ending the silence. For these people, the focus of attention is not on the speaker but rather on their own inner disquiet.[6]

Learning to be comfortable with silence is absolutely essential for pastoral carers. Without the ability to be silent comfortably and easily, carers too often interrupt the flow of the care recipient's thoughts with advice, stories, or other words that ease the carers' discomfort with the silence. These interruptions are deeply disempowering. Silence on the part of listeners is both comforting and empowering.

Skills that Guide Conversations

The ability to guide conversations is also key in pastoral care. We guide conversations so we can get information. We steer conversations in certain directions so we can clarify and understand the issues in a person's life and what that person considers to be important, which helps us understand their life and often helps them discover what really matters to them.

We can direct conversations toward the other person's perception of the intersection between ordinary daily life and God, faith, prayer, spirituality, or something that calls us beyond ourselves. We can encourage people to talk about the ways they are already praying about their situation.

When we guide conversations toward people's views of their own situation, we indicate our interest in their experience and perceptions. We show that we care about what they think and feel, which communicates love and empathy. If we express genuine interest in the way other people view their lives, we empower them to believe their lives matter and they may be able to find solutions from their own inner wisdom.

We guide conversations two ways, by using questions and reflecting. Both questions and reflecting keep people talking, so they meet the needs described above, but questions and reflecting also steer conversations in specific directions.

Questions

Good questions are usually open-ended, which means that they seem to be asking for a sentence or paragraph, rather than one word. "How many siblings do you have?" is a closed question, while "What are your siblings like?" is an open question. In many settings, closed questions work fine to kick off or guide a conversation,

> Good questions are usually open-ended, which means that they seem to be asking for a sentence or paragraph, rather than one word.

Holy listening demands vigilance, alertness, openness to others, and the expectation that God will speak through them. Holy listening trusts that the Holy Spirit acts in and through our listening. We discern and discover the wisdom and will of God by listening to one another and to ourselves. From a Christian perspective, holy listening also takes the incarnation seriously; it dares to believe that, as God was enfleshed in Jesus of Nazareth, so God is embodied in other people and in the things around us.

—Craig Satterlee, "Holy and Active Listening"[7]

because many people are so eager for a listening ear that they will answer even closed questions with a paragraph.

Many statements that are not technically questions function as questions:

- "Tell me more."
- "Help me understand how you decided to do that."
- "I'm interested in hearing more."

These statements are useful in(avoiding "why" questions) which often feel judgmental, aggressive, or intrusive. I was taught in school to ask what, where, when, why, and how questions. All of those work well to guide conversations except why.

Other kinds of questions can also feel intrusive or overwhelming to speakers. I once asked a question that obviously came across as invasive. I was trying to go deeper in a conversation with someone who was moving from acquaintance to friend, and I said, "Where has God been in your life recently?"

She replied, "Wow, you ask hard questions." I apologized to her for sounding intrusive and added that our time together that day was short, so I was jumping in deep because I wanted to give her the opportunity to talk about anything meaningful to her. She seemed fine with my apology, and the conversation did move quite a bit deeper after that interchange. Listeners need to be careful with questions, but not so afraid of being intrusive that we never ask about deeper issues like values, spirituality, and faith. Sometimes we will get it wrong, and that's okay.

Imagine at coffee hour one Sunday you are listening to Tim, who is getting married next month. Tim is talking about the wedding preparations, and he's a bit impatient with his fiancée, Julie, because of her apparent obsession with every detail of the wedding. Mixed into his words is optimism about the marriage after all this wedding nonsense is over.

A follow-up question will steer the conversation. A question like "What have been the hardest parts of your relationship lately?" gives Tim permission to talk about the challenges he's experiencing. If you want to steer Tim into a positive direction you might ask: "What has been the best part of the engagement period?" If you want to guide Tim to questions of faith, you might ask, "How have you experienced God's guidance in the preparation for your marriage?"

〈Asking questions in conversations exerts quite a bit of power, *IHPT* because the question asker is choosing the direction for the conversation.〉When we ask questions, we need to be aware of the presuppositions and values that influence the questions we ask. A question about how people are praying for a situation indicates that we expect them to be people who pray, which is entirely appropriate in some settings but not in others. We need to seek God's guidance for the most fruitful direction for our questions.

Reflecting

Reflecting steers conversations by using statements about what we are hearing and seeing as we listen.〈Choosing what to reflect will also guide the conversation in a certain direction〉Do you reflect back something about Tim's impatience? "You sound frustrated," or "The preparations require so much of Julie's time." Reflecting in that way encourages Tim to vent his irritation, which may be exactly what Tim needs.

great

Ignatian spirituality emphasizes consolation and desolation in prayer and discernment. These concepts can be helpful in using listening skills to guide conversations in pastoral care. Do I want to use questions and reflection to encourage the speaker to talk about desolation, those feelings of sadness, frustration, and loss that everyone needs to talk about sometimes? Or do I want to guide care recipients to focus on consolation, the ways they have experienced joys, blessings, gifts, and sources of energy? I can also use questions and reflecting to encourage my conversation partner to talk about feeling God's presence or absence in consolation and desolation.

Another option for reflection is to pick up on Tim's optimism. "You sound excited about marrying Julie," or "You're looking forward to married life." Perhaps giving Tim the opportunity to talk about his hopes for the marriage will empower him to feel less irritated by Julie's absorption in the details. The choice of what to reflect makes a big difference in where the conversation heads.

Note that reflecting involves making a statement, not asking a question. I've taught numerous listening workshops, and when I ask people to practice reflecting, most of them ask questions. Questions are essential to good listening, but reflecting is something different.

The reflecting I've illustrated above involves a statement that summarizes or paraphrases what the listener thinks the speaker has said or what we think the speaker's tone of voice or body language are communicating. An additional form of reflecting involves simply repeating the last few words the speaker has said. This sometimes feels quite mechanical when doing it, but it works well to keep speakers talking without guiding them.

One more form of reflecting involves drawing an implication or connection that the speaker hasn't expressed. When the listener is able to provide an insight the speaker hasn't thought of, the listener gives a big gift to the speaker. Some of the possible implications that could be drawn from what Tim has said include:

- "You wonder if Julie's preoccupation with the wedding will have a lasting impact on your relationship."
- "You feel both frustration and optimism, and you wonder which one will predominate when you're married."
- "You have questions about where God is in the midst of all the emotions you're experiencing."

Tim may say, "Yes, you're right, I hadn't thought of it that way." Or he may say, "I'm still confident our marriage will be great, but I want to get the wedding over with." When we draw implications, we have to be humble, because we could be completely wrong. In fact, one of the purposes of reflecting is to clarify whether we have

Activities?

Yes!

Reflecting steers conversations by using statements about what we are hearing and seeing as we listen.

p. 131
→ Accurate info.

heard correctly. If we've made a mistake in what we thought we were hearing, the other person can clarify, which can be helpful to both listener and speaker.

Reflecting is empowering to the speaker in several ways. Reflecting [1] indicates that the problem belongs to the speaker, in contrast with giving advice, which implies that the listener knows more about the situation than the speaker does. Reflecting keeps the conversation [2] focused on the speaker, which helps the listener avoid falling into a role of rescuer.

Reflecting helps speakers clarify their own thinking about the [3] issue at hand. As they hear listeners summarize the issues, speakers sometimes see the situation in a new light. Sometimes when we use reflecting, we get the situation wrong, and the speaker says, "No, that's not what I meant." When we accept that statement and say, "Oh, tell me what you did mean," we give power back to the speaker.

When used wisely and with compassion, asking questions and reflecting show empathy, another significant listening skill.

Empathy

It may seem odd to consider empathy as a skill. Yet, we can definitely grow in our ability to empathize, and working on specific behaviors helps us empathize more deeply, so in that sense it fits into the category of skill.

A communication textbook gives this definition: Empathy is the cognitive process of identifying with or vicariously experiencing the feelings, thoughts, or attitudes of another. . . . When we empathize, we are attempting to understand and/or experience what another person understands and/or experiences.[8]

If empathy is a cognitive process, then we can work on strengthening our ability to use our brains in that way. According to

> Empathy is the cognitive process of identifying with or vicariously experiencing the feelings, thoughts, or attitudes of another.

the definition, this cognitive process has several components. When practicing empathy, we attempt to:

- Identify with
- Experience feelings, thoughts, and attitudes
- Understand

The first time I taught a class on chaplaincy, we discussed this definition. My students engaged in a spirited conversation about whether empathy is possible. One student argued that empathy is impossible and that we need to be honest about that. We absolutely cannot, he said, experience what another person experiences. The other students stressed that the key word in this definition is "attempting." All we can do is *attempt to* identify, experience, and understand, but we must attempt it. Christian love demands that we try.

Two communication scholars suggest that if we want to empathize, we can ask ourselves two questions: "What emotions do I believe the person is experiencing right now?" and "What are the cues the person is giving that I am using to draw this conclusion?"[9]

Empathy, then, can be increased by trying to figure out what people feel about what they are saying. These feelings can sometimes be observed in body language, and we can use reflecting to check on whether our perceptions are accurate, perhaps saying something like, "You seem quite tense today" or "Your face has a sad expression today." Asking questions about feelings can also help the person to talk about their inner realities, and then we can attempt to identify, experience, and understand those.

Empathy starts with taking people and their concerns seriously, so the listening skills I've described here can help nurture empathy: keeping people talking by using body language, minimal encouragers, and silence, and guiding conversations with questions and reflecting. These foundational listening skills express that we care about another person's reality.

> As God's chosen ones, holy and beloved, clothe yourselves with compassion, kindness, humility, meekness and patience. Bear with one another.
>
> —Colossians 3:12–13

Recently I've seen a flurry of activity online in blog posts and videos about the difference between sympathy and empathy.[10] Sympathy is feeling compassion, sorrow, or pity for another person, and empathy involves trying to feel what the other person is feeling. Perhaps sympathy comes in two forms, one of which is paternalistic and full of the kind of pity that puts one person up and the other person down. That kind of sympathy creates dependence, and the online material I've been seeing is scathing about how nasty sympathy is when it takes this form.

I think there's a form of sympathy that is compassionate, in which I acknowledge to myself that I'm not willing or able to try to feel what the other person is feeling, but I do care or want to care. Compassionate sympathy, while falling short of empathy, seems to me to be much better than indifference.

In the Gospel of Matthew, Jesus is described as having compassion four times. Luke mentions compassion in the story of the prodigal son, where the father saw his son returning and "was filled with compassion" (Luke 15:20).

I watched a production of *Godspell* where the father saw the son across the stage and pulled a Frisbee out of his shirt. The Frisbee had a big heart on it, and the father threw the Frisbee to the son. The father's heart went out to the son, a metaphorical way of illustrating compassion. Compassion and empathy are closely related as we try to understand and identify with others.

Contrasts in Listening

All the listening skills I've described help conversations go deeper, and I love deep conversations. I've always been a bit impatient with conversations about the weather. Why can't we talk about something more significant?

Eight years ago, in preparation to teach the course on chaplaincy, I read several communication textbooks to find material on listening for my students. One of those textbooks had a section entitled "Contrasts in Listening," where the authors described some contrasts that good listeners keep in mind. The first contrast helped me understand weather conversation.

✓ *Deep and Surface Listening*

Deep listening requires intense focus, a lot of time, and careful use of a variety of listening skills to help the speaker express thoughts, feelings, and emotions. Surface listening invites casual conversation about things like the weather. Because of the effort and energy required to listen deeply, casual conversations involving surface listening are a helpful way to connect with people in many everyday settings, conveying ease and acceptance without spending the energy and time necessary for deep listening.

In pastoral care settings, good listeners use both deep and surface listening in the appropriate situations. Maybe a little weather conversation in a pastoral care conversation will help the care recipient relax. Maybe some discussion of sports or vacations will help care recipients decide I'm trustworthy. Then perhaps later we can go deeper.

✓ *Participatory and Passive Listening*

Sometimes the speaker is talking fluidly, and the listener can sit back and let the speaker talk. The speaker is talking through the issues and making headway in finding wisdom to deal with challenges. In that instance, no listening skills are required other than silence, and the style of listening is passive. Other times, lots of questions and reflecting are necessary to draw out speakers or to help them focus on the issue at hand, and the style of listening is participatory, which requires focus, wise use of listening skills, and a lot of energy. In pastoral care settings, good listeners pay attention to cues indicating when to spend a lot of energy using a variety of listening skills and when to relax a bit and let the conversation flow on its own.

In pastoral care settings, good listeners use both deep and surface listening in the appropriate situations.

✓ *Empathetic and Objective Listening*

Empathy conveys love in a powerful way, while objective listening helps get the facts on the table. Imagine talking to a care recipient who is facing eviction from his apartment. Empathetic listening helps the man express his feelings. When trying to get the details regarding the eviction in order to provide practical help, though, a focus on objective facts is necessary. In pastoral care settings, ✓ good listeners move between empathetic listening, when people's emotions are engaged, and objective listening, when problems are being discussed.[11]

This third contrast is a bit different from the other two because even in the midst of empathy, some degree of objectivity is required. Objectivity is necessary to think clearly about which direction might be the most helpful to the person speaking. Listeners need to remain objective as we deliberate about which listening skills will convey empathy most effectively.

Objectivity is also necessary for us to observe and deal with what's going inside of us as we listen. Some people use the term "inner noise" to describe the various emotions and thoughts we feel as we listen. The anxiety raised by these emotions and thoughts is the biggest obstacle to listening.

> One of the primary tasks of the listener is to stay out of the other's way so the listener can discover how the speaker views his situation.
>
> —Robert Bolton, "Listening Is More Than Merely Hearing"[12]

Inner Noise

Many things can distract us from listening well. The term "outer noise" is sometimes used to describe the situations that impede listening: a noisy room, a second conversation close by, a chaotic setting, or background music. "Inner noise" describes the emotions and thoughts that can get in the way of listening. These include thoughts and feelings we bring into a conversation with us, such as absorption about something scheduled for later in the day or the long to-do list crowding our minds.

Here's the question I get asked most often about listening: "How do I cope with people who won't stop talking?" Listeners can attempt to guide such conversations beyond details into meaning, faith, and deep reflection. Listeners can stop the person speaking and say, "I'd like to pray for you now, based on what you've already said." Sometimes conversation after a prayer is more focused and less frantic. Listeners can establish a time limit in their own mind, and perhaps state that limit out loud, and stop the conversation when the time is up, even if the person is still talking. Very talkative people are challenging, and carers can brainstorm with other carers about coping strategies and how to set limits.

Inner noise can also come from our reactions to what our conversation partner is saying. Once again, imagine that conversation with Tim, who is experiencing both irritation and hopeful anticipation as he approaches his wedding. Maybe you had a tumultuous build-up to your own wedding, and Tim's words bring back a lot of painful memories. Maybe you know Tim's parents, and you know they really don't like his fiancée, so as Tim talks, you're worried about his parents' emotions. Or maybe you know that Tim and his fiancée are living together, and you believe that's a bad way to start a marriage, and your disapproval fills your mind.

Coping with inner noise—including the to-do list, memories, worries, and judgments—is a key listening skill. The first step in dealing with it wisely is to recognize that everyone experiences an astonishing array of thoughts and feelings as they listen. Communication scholars use the term "double listening" to describe the need to listen to the conversation partner while also paying attention to our own thoughts and feelings as we listen.

SKILL #1

A friend who teaches counseling told me that the major skill addressed in the first six months of counseling training involves learning to cope with inner noise. He said he suggests to students that they imagine a parking lot, and every time they experience a thought or emotion that distracts them from listening, they park that thought or feeling over in the parking lot.

SKILL #2

In some instances, simply parking the inner noise makes it go away. In other instances, after the conversation has finished, we need to take the inner noise out of the parking lot and try to figure out what was going on inside of us during that portion of the conversation.

Habitual Responses to Inner Noise

Inner noise derails conversations in predictable ways. If our thoughts and feelings create anxiety as we listen, we usually have a favorite way of making sure the anxiety goes away. In a communications textbook, Richard Bolstad and Margot Hamblett describe behaviors we fall into habitually when we feel uneasy in a conversation:

[handwritten margin note: Imptl Key to recognize]

- Giving advice or moralizing. Solution giving taps into our need to take action, to be practical and strategize.
- Judging. Judgments often arise from anxiety. "Why" questions can derail listening because they can imply judgment.
- Denying. Listeners sometimes use praise or reassurance as a way to deny a problem exists. "It will work out." "You're so smart, you'll figure it out."
- Interrogating. Too many questions can have the opposite effect of what was intended. The barrage of questions can make the speaker feel defensive, exposed, and distracted from the main issue.[13]
- Redirecting the conversation toward action. "Let's get those dishes done." "We talked about going for a walk. Why don't we do that now?"
- Telling a parallel story at length. When listening to someone talk about a death in the family, it might be appropriate to talk briefly about our own recent experience of grief. But taking the story back from the other person to talk at length about our own situation usually comes from uncomfortable inner noise.

Most listeners have a favorite behavior on the list above. For me, I easily default into giving advice. These responses lessen the discomfort that inner noise raises in us, the listeners, helping us feel less anxious about the situation. The negative emotions in the listener—anxiety or discomfort—are thus transferred to the speaker, who now has to cope with the original situation along with the new emotions raised by the listener's response. The listener, then, adds to the speaker's burden, which is profoundly disempowering.

Grieving with Others

Good illustration narrative

I've learned a lot about listening in the past two and a half years, since my husband, Dave, developed a chronic lung disease originally diagnosed as a fungal infection. Before the illness, he was one of the most physically fit people I knew.

The first year was a blur of constant infections, numerous medical tests, and three nasty months on an antifungal drug with horrendous side effects. The horrible drug sent his fungal infection into remission. In the second year, he settled into an adjustment phase where he had to adapt to having less energy, intermittent bacterial lung infections, and constant discomfort in his lungs. Our relatives, friends, the church staff, and many other people in our lives know about Dave's chronic illness.

I have watched countless people express care to Dave in the past two and a half years. Typically what happens is that people ask Dave how he's doing. They listen patiently to Dave's brief initial answer. Both the question and the attentive listening communicate empathy.

This moment of empathy, however, is usually very short. I am astonished at how few people encourage Dave to keep talking by using body language, minimal encouragers, or silence. I am equally astonished by how few follow up by asking a question about how he's coping or by reflecting back what they've heard to encourage him to say more.

After the initial question, Dave's brief response, and their words of sympathy, people almost always do one of three things: give advice about how to strengthen his immune system ("Have you tried Echinacea?" "Do you take Vitamin C?"), tell him a long story about someone they know who had a chronic illness, or change the subject.

> You must understand this, my beloved: let everyone be quick to listen.
>
> —James 1:19

Days and sometimes weeks go by where I am the only person who encourages Dave to talk about how he's feeling emotionally and spiritually in the midst of this illness. Sometimes I think I'm the only one who is willing to spend more than one or two minutes focused on Dave and what Dave has to say about his situation. I find this both astonishing and deeply frustrating.

Why would people find it so difficult to invite Dave to say more about how he is feeling physically and emotionally and how he is coping? Many people worry about asking invasive questions. People also often feel a strong need to be helpful and to fix difficult situations. Chronic diseases are not fixable. In chapter 1, I quoted Henri Nouwen's words about friends who "can tolerate not-knowing, not-curing, not-healing and face with us the reality of our powerlessness."[14] Our need to know, cure, and heal is a form of inner noise that creates major roadblocks to listening.

Nouwen believes that the basic meaning of the word "care" is to lament with another person, "to grieve, to experience sorrow, to cry out with."[15] The next time someone tells you about something hard in their life—perhaps a health issue, a job conflict, a challenging family relationship, or a financial problem—do an experiment. Respond with these words, "I'm so sorry to hear about this," and then stop talking.

Wait and see what happens next. While you wait, try to empathize. Attempt to identify with the person; attempt to experience the feelings, thoughts, and attitudes they might be experiencing; and attempt to understand.

If you want to have one useful follow-up question in your tool box, try this: "How is that for you?" The person with the difficult situation can go any direction and can talk briefly or at length.

So many people are waiting for a listener to grieve with them.

Triple Listening

In order to avoid responding in a knee-jerk way that impedes listening, we need to be attentive to the other person's words and body language and also to our own thoughts and feelings, the inner noise that can impede listening. That's a form of double listening. Christians have an additional challenge. We need to listen for God's guidance in conversations as well. Perhaps then, for Christian carers, we might talk about triple listening: listening to another person, our own inner reality, and God.

SKILL #3

Listening to God and trying to rely on God's guidance as we converse helps us make wise choices about how to guide conversations as we deploy the skills of asking questions and reflecting. Every question or reflection takes a conversation in a certain direction, but is it the direction God desires for the conversation?

Empathy requires the cognitive effort of trying to observe the cues that communicate what the person is thinking and feeling. Empathy involves attempting to identify and understand. Surely God's guidance is needed for these challenges. We also need God's help to be honest about the thoughts and feelings that can derail us as we listen.

Training Tips

If you lead training sessions for pastoral carers,

1. Give them opportunities to brainstorm the kinds of questions that open up faith issues.

2. Give them time to practice reflecting, one of the most challenging skills to learn, using actual stories and scenarios.

3. Help participants explore the ways inner noise shuts down listening for them.

4. Discuss "triple listening," focusing on what helps carers listen on three levels simultaneously.

This chapter has emphasized the ways listening can empower others, but there are times to speak as well as listen. Sometimes a story from our own lives or a story from the Bible is exactly the right thing. Sometimes compassionate words are helpful. We need to listen to God's guidance for when and how to speak up, and we need to pay attention to our own inner wisdom about what is happening in the conversation.

Most people need to talk less and listen more.

However, most people need to talk less and listen more. Many pastoral carers need to grow in listening skills that guide conversations in directions that are helpful for care recipients, providing opportunities that enable care recipients to find their own wisdom for coping with their challenges.

Listening skills for pastoral carers are more essential than ever because of the many changes in pastoral care described in the first half of this book. Teamwork among carers and empowerment of care recipients is greatly enhanced by good listening skills. Helpful service to people from other countries and with diverse ethnic backgrounds demands a significant commitment to listening. Building relationships with people outside the congregation requires good listening skills. Listening undergirds pastoral care in the twenty-first century more than ever.

VITAL

For Reflection and Discussion

1 What are the situations where silence is most difficult for you in conversations? Do you have ideas about why that is the case?

2 What are the biggest obstacles for you as you try to empathize? How have you tried to overcome them?

3 What forms of inner noise most often derail your ability to listen? How do you most often shut down listening? How have you tried to grow in this area?

4 When you think of triple listening—listening to another person, to your own thoughts and feelings, and to God—what do you

find most challenging? Most encouraging? Write a prayer for yourself as a listener, and be sure to thank God for the people who listen to you.

Resources

Baab, Lynne M. *The Power of Listening: Building Skills for Mission and Ministry*. Lanham, MD: Rowman & Littlefield, 2014.

> My book on listening lays out the material in this chapter in more detail and also addresses patterns of listening in congregational settings including pastoral care, congregational discernment, and local outreach.

McHugh, Adam S. *The Listening Life: Embracing Attentiveness in a World of Distraction*. Downers Grove, IL: InterVarsity, 2015.

> McHugh's chapter on listening to people in pain will be helpful to carers, as will his reflections on attentiveness to God and the challenges of listening in our noisy world.

Hart, Thomas N. *The Art of Christian Listening*. New York: Paulist, 1980.

> Drawing on Jungian psychology, Hart presents the significance of listening for Christians, especially spiritual directors. His emphasis on listening as helping and holy will be relevant for pastoral carers.

Brown, Brené. "Brené Brown on Empathy vs Sympathy." YouTube video, 2:53. Uploaded by "Diana Simon Psihoterapeut," April 1, 2016. https://tinyurl.com/y8u3gvvg.

> A wonderful presentation on empathy. I disagree with her view of sympathy. What she calls "sympathy," I would call paternalistic advice-giving.

10
Spiritual Practices

I AM twenty-two years old, beginning a new job in campus ministry. A student is telling me about her painful breakup with her boyfriend. After we talk, I want to pray for her, but I'm unsure how to suggest it. She gets up to leave for her next class, and I feel that I have let her down by not initiating prayer.

Fast forward four decades, and I am listening to a young woman talk about the stress she experiences in her job. The setting is coffee hour after church, and I now feel confident in saying, "Would you like me to say a quick prayer for you?" She says "yes" with a sigh of relief. Despite the people and conversations around us, I put my hand on her shoulder and pray briefly for her.

Fast forward a couple of weeks, and I'm sitting in my office at the university with a woman in her midlife years who is studying part-time and working part-time in a church. I use my objective listening skills as we brainstorm essay topics.

I know her pretty well after several semesters, so I ask her how she's doing as she balances work, study, and family. Suddenly we're in pastoral care mode as she tells me about her intense and varied feelings about a male coworker. She's feeling sexual attraction for the coworker, fear about her attraction, gratitude for her husband in many ways, yet frustration with her marriage in some other areas. I want to pray with her in the most helpful way possible.

I am now, after four decades in various ministry positions, confident in suggesting prayer and leading people into prayer, but I still have questions in my mind. What is the best form of prayer for this woman? Intercessory prayer focused on the issues she has expressed? Some other form of prayer, perhaps breath prayer, where I make a space for her to relinquish her negative and fearful feelings into God's presence?

I could invite her to confess the aspects of her emotions and behaviors that she believes are sinful, in order to receive God's forgiveness. I could lead her into a guided meditation, which might help her meet Jesus and talk with him about her emotions. Perhaps I should combine one or two of these forms of prayer.

Maybe I should use the Bible as a resource. We could pray a psalm together, perhaps a psalm that expresses sorrow for sin. We could read the story of Jesus healing the bent-over woman in Luke 13:10–17. This woman I'm talking with certainly seems burdened by her feelings—bent over metaphorically—and maybe the story would precipitate some ideas about how to pray for this situation. Or we could read one of the apostle Paul's prayers and pray the words for her.

I decide to read parts of Psalm 91 to her. Then I ask if she wants to pray about her situation. She says yes, and both of us pray aloud.

A significant aspect of Christian pastoral care is praying with care recipients, guiding them to appropriate passages in the Bible, and helping them develop their own patterns of drawing near to God. In addition, Christian pastoral carers need to come to their ministry with the foundation of knowing we are beloved of God, with an expectation of God's presence in every care situation. Spiritual practices can help us hold on to that perspective. Therefore, pastoral carers must have an understanding of and commitment to spiritual practices and feel comfortable talking about them with care recipients.

yes!

foundational

Christian pastoral carers need to come to their ministry with the foundation of knowing we are beloved of God, with an expectation of God's presence in every care situation. Spiritual practices can help us hold on to that perspective. Pastoral carers must have an understanding of and commitment to spiritual practices and feel comfortable talking about them with care recipients.

What Are Spiritual Practices?

Spiritual practices, also called spiritual disciplines, were neglected for three-quarters of the twentieth century in many Christian settings. Richard Foster brought them back to the attention of Protestants in the West with his landmark 1978 book, *A Celebration of Discipline.*[1] I have conducted well over a hundred interviews for my books on spiritual practices, and Foster's book was mentioned by more interviewees than all other books combined.

Spiritual practices enable us to respond to two of the great themes of the New Testament: God is present with us, and God calls us to be transformed.

God's Presence

God is present with us in Christ through the Holy Spirit. In chapter 3, when discussing the ministry of presence, I mentioned God's presence with many individuals in the Hebrew Scriptures and God's presence with us through the incarnation of Jesus. Jesus promised his disciples he would return to them in the Holy Spirit: "I will not leave you orphaned; I am coming to you" (John 14:18). Jesus's last words in the Gospel of Matthew reflect the same promise: "And remember, I am with you always, to the end of the age" (Matt 28:20).

Adele Ahlberg Calhoun, a spiritual director and copastor of a church in Massachusetts, fleshes out the connection between God's presence and spiritual practices. She describes more than sixty spiritual practices in her helpful *Spiritual Disciplines Handbook.*

The word discipline means "the effort to create some space in which God can act." Discipline means to prevent everything in your life from being filled up . . . to create that space in which something can happen that you hadn't planned or counted on.

—Henri Nouwen, referring to spiritual disciplines in "Moving from Solitude to Community to Ministry"[2]

Calhoun defines spiritual disciplines as intentional practices, relationships, and experiences that give people space to "keep company" with Jesus. Calhoun's words show the close connection between the terms *disciplines* and *practices*, which means that most people use *spiritual disciplines* and *spiritual practices* interchangeably.

Calhoun emphasizes the relational aspect of spiritual practices. When we engage in any spiritual practice, we are making space in our lives so we can experience the God who is already present with us. When we go to church, pray with a friend, open a Bible, keep the Sabbath, or write thankfulness prayers in a journal, we "keep company with Jesus."

When we do those things, we expect—or at least hope—to encounter God. We want to be with Jesus. We want to perceive the large or small nudging of the Holy Spirit, who makes God's presence with us possible. We often come to spiritual practices out of our own need, perhaps wanting God's comfort, guidance, support, hope, peace, or joy in the midst of the challenges of daily life. As Calhoun writes, we do these things because of the "desire for more of God."[4]

God's Transformation

A second description of spiritual practices draws on the common New Testament theme of transformation. Marjorie Thompson's 1997 book, *Soul Feast: An Invitation to the Christian Spiritual Life*, was one of the first major books on spiritual practices after Richard Foster's.

Thompson describes her goal in writing the book: "My purpose is to help people of faith understand and begin to practice some of the basic disciplines of the Christian spiritual life. Disciplines are simply practices that train us in faithfulness."[5] Again, her words show the overlap between "disciplines" and "practices." She discusses seven areas of spiritual disciplines: reading Scripture, prayer, worship, fasting, confession/self-examination, spiritual direction, and hospitality.

> The Lord of Hosts is with us; the God of Jacob is our refuge.
>
> —Psalm 46:7

According to Thompson, spiritual practices train us in faithfulness. As we study the Bible, we learn how to be faithful to God. Over time, as we pray, confess our sins, engage in hospitality, and make space in our lives in various ways to "keep company with Jesus," we become more faithful.

Thompson goes on to say, "Such practices have consistently been experienced as vehicles of God's presence, guidance, and call in the lives of faithful seekers."[6] While we are being trained, we are also experiencing God's presence, guidance, and call. God's presence with us and God's shaping of us are intricately connected.

This theme of transformation occurs in numerous places in the New Testament. The apostle Paul writes, "Do not be conformed to this world but be transformed by the renewing of your minds, so that you may discern what is the will of God—what is good and acceptable and perfect" (Rom 12:2). How do we discern the will of God? By reading the Bible, by praying for God's guidance, by slowing down our lives enough to hear God's still small voice. In other words, by making space in our lives to keep company with Jesus.

Many writers on spiritual practices propose categories in order to help people explore the diversity of options. I find these three categories to be helpful:

1 Prayer, which includes many different ways of drawing near to God: spoken, silent, sung, individual, communal, liturgical, extemporaneous, praise, confession, thankfulness, petition, lament, and so forth.

2 Engaging with the Bible, which includes many options: reading, study, reflection, meditation, memorization, Scripture, songs, and the like.

3 Other, which includes corporate worship, Sabbath, fasting, journaling, simplicity, retreats, small groups, spiritual direction, stewardship, hospitality, and so on. Note that many options in this category include prayer and the Bible or make space for the option of prayer or Scripture reading.

The theme of training as a part of transformation is mentioned several times in the New Testament. The Christian life is referred to as a race several times in the Epistles (see 1 Cor 9:24 and 2 Tim 4:7).

The writer of the letter to the Hebrews develops the metaphor of a race further: "Let us run with perseverance the race that is set before us, looking to Jesus, the pioneer and perfecter of our faith" (Heb 12:1–2). For Christians, running the race involves keeping our eyes on Jesus, which takes us back to the notion of Jesus's presence with us.

✱ Presence and Transformation in Pastoral Care

These two themes of spiritual practices—the presence of God with us and God's work of transformation in us—are also two central themes of pastoral care. When we provide pastoral care, we hope that our presence, words, and actions will reassure care recipients that God is with them. Pastoral care at its best opens up spaces for people to talk about the overlap between their daily lives and their sense of God or the sacred. Why is that overlap possible? Because God is with us.

In pastoral care, we do our best to enable others to experience God's presence with them no matter what the situation. We help people learn to bring their cares and concerns to God in prayer. We pray with and for care recipients, because God is with us, longing to show love to us.

In addition, we pray with and for care recipients because God longs to help us grow and change. We try to help carers in a multitude of ways, including prayer, that contribute to their transformation into the people they were created to be.

Christian pastoral carers need to understand and engage in spiritual practices themselves so they will be able to pray and use the Bible wisely in pastoral care settings and discuss spiritual practices with care recipients. In addition, and even more importantly, Christian pastoral carers need a sense of God's empowering, rooted in God's

Yes!.

These two themes of spiritual practices—the presence of God with us and God's work of transformation in us— are also two central themes of pastoral care.

> For we do not have a high priest who is unable to sympathize with our weaknesses, but we have one who in every respect has been tested as we are, yet without sin. Let us therefore approach the throne of grace, with boldness, so that we may receive mercy and find grace to help in time of need.
>
> —Hebrews 4:15–16

love, in order to provide pastoral care with a uniquely Christian emphasis.

In pastoral care, we do helping acts that contribute to care recipients in seven areas: healing, sustaining, guiding, reconciling, nurturing, liberating, and empowering. As carers, we cannot do these actions without God's presence with us for support and transformation.

7 verbs p.23

In addition, each time we provide help in one of these ways, we ourselves are transformed a bit more into the image of the One who exemplifies these actions. We serve after the model of Jesus, and when we copy someone, over time we are shaped and transformed, and we become more like that person.

?.

In the remainder of this chapter I will first discuss the way Christian carers can use prayer and the Bible in pastoral care settings. Then I will focus on the foundational truth that carers need to be deeply grounded in Christian spiritual practices in order to serve God effectively in pastoral care ministries.

Prayer in Pastoral Care Settings

As I illustrated at the beginning of this chapter, prayer in pastoral care settings can take many forms, and the most common is intercessory prayer. It might begin with the carer's question, "Would you like me to pray for you?" If the answer is yes, then the carer can pray a simple extemporaneous prayer that draws on what the care recipient has said. I usually leave some silence at the end in case the

What would you like to pray for/about?

other person wants to pray out loud as well. Becoming confident in this form of prayer is essential for carers.

Many of my students have been chaplains who serve in a variety of secular settings such as hospitals, nursing homes, and prisons, and most of them ask all care recipients if they would like to be prayed for. My students told me that most people seem eager to receive prayer, even if two minutes earlier they were talking about why they aren't people of faith.

In addition to extemporaneous intercessory prayers, many other forms of prayer are appropriate in pastoral care settings, including:

- Liturgical or printed prayers
- Thankfulness prayers
- Lament prayers
- Silent prayers
- Guided meditations
- Inner-healing prayers
- Mindfulness meditations
- Breath prayers

Tradition's
? minister/pastor/chaplain
prayer book

I am particularly fond of breath prayer. The simplest form of breath prayer is to use each out breath as an opportunity to breathe out problems and challenges into the presence of God, and to use each in breath to imagine breathing in God's love. In God "we live and move and have our being" (Acts 17:28), so God surrounds us like the air we breathe. When I explain this to care recipients, I usually tell them I'll give them thirty seconds, about ten breaths, or a minute, about twenty breaths.

Another simple form of breath prayer is to use a prayer that the person already knows, such as the Lord's Prayer or the Jesus Prayer, and ask them to pray the prayer silently, with a phrase for each breath. Another option is to ask the person to pick two or three names or characteristics for God or Jesus and then to sit silently, maybe for a minute or two, saying one name or characteristic on each breath.

Praying with our breath slows down our breathing, which slows down many of the functions of our body. In this stressful and fast-paced world, even one minute of slowing down can be so soothing. The sense of peace that comes from slowing our breathing can put problems into a more hopeful perspective.

The Bible in Pastoral Care

My most recent spiritual director was a Roman Catholic Dominican sister. Her own spiritual practice included reading the lectionary passages every morning. In about half of our monthly meetings over the three years I saw her for spiritual direction, she would say something like this, "What you've just described reminds me of the passage in Mark I read this morning." Then she would pull out her Bible, read me part or all of the passage, and tell me how she felt it related to what I had said.

Her pattern of reading a passage from the Bible to me accomplished several things. It modeled the spiritual practice of daily Scripture reading. It turned my attention to God, and helped me to see my life in the light of that specific incident or teaching in the Bible. It helped me see my situation from a new perspective, because I would certainly not have made a connection between my life and the passages she chose.

Some pastoral carers follow the model of my spiritual director and cite passages they have read recently. Other pastoral carers assemble

Parts of the Bible particularly relevant for carers include:

- The Psalms, the prayer book of the Bible, which presents just about every human emotion. Praying psalms is a great way to make the emotions in them more real and immediate and to experience God's presence in the midst of those emotions.
- The Gospels, which present Jesus's pattern of ministry, a model for our ministry in so many ways.
- The apostle Paul's prayers, at the beginning of many of his letters. We can pray his prayers for ourselves and for others.

a mental or written list of passages that work well in various situations, maybe a handful of psalms that address various forms of grief and stress and another group of New Testament passages that are encouraging or challenging. Either way, pastoral carers need to engage in some depth with the passages before reading them with care recipients, so the carer can share how the Scripture applies.

The two themes I mentioned earlier about spiritual practices and pastoral care—God with us and God transforming us—are helpful themes to think about when choosing biblical passages to use in pastoral care. Pointing out or reading passages that speak to those two themes often helps care recipients be reminded of God's goodness to them.

Discussing Spiritual Practices

In addition to praying with care recipients, carers may want to ask some questions about the care recipients' own prayer life or other spiritual practices. Almost every time I speak on spiritual practices or have a conversation with an individual about spiritual practices, I hear: "I don't pray or read the Bible enough." Whenever I speak on the Sabbath, I get, "I should keep a Sabbath."

I have wondered whether these responses indicate that people really don't keep company with Jesus very often, or whether they feel insecure talking about the ways they do experience God's presence. So I usually start asking questions, such as, "Tell me the places and times you feel close to God."

I want to figure out several things. Which spiritual practices does the person already engage in? How could those be developed further? Which new practices might the person try? Rather than starting with advice, a discussion of spiritual practices can begin with times and activities in care recipients' lives when they already experience God's presence and God's transformation.

I love Calhoun's *Spiritual Disciplines Handbook* because it lists so many specific and diverse spiritual practices. Looking over all those

~~Meatballs~~
~~Grits~~
~~Collards~~

Globes
Judas : the Black
Messiah

Mauritanian
J. Foster

Trial of Chicago 7

TV. I Know this
Much Is True

options can help a carer see the things that people are already doing that function as spiritual practices for them. The carer can encourage further development of those practices, which often seems much more doable than starting something new.

Further development of an existing practice, no matter how small, breaks up that negative self-talk, "I don't pray or read the Bible enough." Pastoral carers need to discuss spiritual practices with care recipients in a way that empowers them, which is tricky in a climate of guilt and self-deprecation. God's grace must be the foundation, and God's presence with us and love for us are essential topics to include in the discussion.

Sometimes it feels appropriate to introduce the option of new spiritual practices. To the person who is stressed from being on the go all the time, discussing the possibility of a Sabbath might be appropriate. For those who are anxious, various forms of contemplative prayer or mindfulness meditation might be helpful, and carers can lead care recipients into those forms of prayer as a part of meeting together. For the person who expresses concern about addiction to a smart phone or social media, a technology fast might be an appropriate suggestion.

Spiritual Practices for Carers

Christians who want to care for others must first receive care from God. Christian pastoral carers must serve, as much as possible, out of a reservoir of love that is frequently replenished by the One who loves us deeply and fully. Spiritual practices make space in our lives for us to walk with Jesus, who loves us and strengthens us so we can love others. Spiritual practices train us in faithfulness, so we can faithfully serve in the ways God calls us to serve.

Earlier I noted that conversations about spiritual practices with care recipients should usually begin with noticing the times and places when they already draw near to God. The same guidance applies to any assessment by carers of our own spiritual practices. Where

Spiritual practices make space in our lives for us to walk with Jesus, who loves us and strengthens us so we can love others. Spiritual practices train us in faithfulness, so we can faithfully serve in the ways God calls us to serve.

① Make space
② Train in faithfulness

(handwritten: 2.)

do I feel companionship with God? When do I experience peace, comfort, worship, and awe in God's presence? What are the habits in my life that contribute to my transformation into Christ's image?

We need to be gentle with ourselves in assessing our spiritual practices. We will be no good to others if we are beating ourselves up about not praying or reading the Bible enough. We read in the Psalms, "The Lord is gracious and merciful, slow to anger and abounding in steadfast love" (Ps 145:8). If God is merciful and slow to anger, who are we to vent anger on ourselves? If we come into a pastoral care conversation filled with shame about our own companionship with Jesus, we will find it quite difficult to convey God's presence and love to a care recipient. *(handwritten: wow!)*

(handwritten: great!) As much as possible, we need to receive God's love and rest in God's acceptance of us, just as we are. This includes not engaging in self-criticism about our faith practices. At the same time, we need to challenge ourselves to draw near to God as much as we can for our own sakes and for the sake of people we care for. *(handwritten: Key → transform make space faithfulness)*

Andrew Purves, a theologian, seminary professor, and Presbyterian minister, wrote a book that looks at pastoral care over the centuries. He describes a theme he sees over and over in classical writing on pastoral care. That theme, he says, is exemplified by the words of Richard Baxter, a seventeenth-century English Puritan, who tells people in ministry: "Take heed to yourself."[8]

Purves focuses on ministers in congregations, but the same words apply to anyone involved in caring for others:

The appeal is not, however, to self-fulfillment, but to disciplined attention to one's life in God. The classical authors understood that unless a pastor within a congregation is within a deepening process of conversion and sanctification, that pastor is in grave danger of both self-deceit and building ministry upon the loose foundation of his or her own unexamined needs.[9]

How does that deepening process happen? In many ways, to be sure, and one of those ways is through spiritual practices. The dangers Purves cites—self-deceit and being motivated by unexamined needs—can be addressed, at least in part, through spiritual practices like meditation on the Bible, journaling, spiritual direction, and many forms of prayer. These practices make space for honesty about the inner forces that motivate us, some of them healthy and some of them not so helpful.

danger!

The carer with a deep need to be needed may look to the care recipient to convey a level of gratitude that the care recipient is simply not able to express. Carers who never got enough attention in childhood may shift the focus in pastoral care sessions onto their own situation, rather than staying focused on the care recipient.

If one goal of pastoral care is to empower others, then carers need to be as sure as we can that our words and actions are not coming from unhealthy places within ourselves, such as unmet needs from childhood or ego-driven drives for attention and power. If our own unmet needs are playing a significant role in the way we care, then we will unconsciously try to meet those needs rather than empower the person we're caring for. Spiritual practices that make room for self-reflection can help avoid unloving behavior that comes from self-deceit.

 Excellent!

Many people in ministry positions pray and study the Bible for the purpose of their work, praying with people in need or with congregational leaders and studying the Bible to preach, lead a Bible study, or lead a devotional time. I recommend that all carers have at

Prayer is not telling God what we think, or simply thanking him for his provision of food and drink. Rather it is our active, intentional effort to understand what God is doing and how we can join him. Thus through prayer we become coparticipants with God. God's will sets everything in motion. Our will, directed by devotion and prayer, allows us to participate in his purposes. Together, prayer and devotion form our inner being.

—Richard Foster and Gayle Beebe, *Longing for God*[10]

Yes! least one prayer practice and one way of engaging with the Bible that have nothing to do with any form of helping anyone else. This affirms that our own journey with God matters just for itself, and that we desire our own transformation into Christ's image.

In chapter 4, I talked about pastoral care as missional, shaped by the God who sent Jesus into the world and who sends us into the world to serve after the model of Jesus. The early morning prayer of Jesus, when he communed with his Father and received guidance for his ministry, gives us a pattern for service that is guided by God day after day. Jesus did what he was called to do and nothing more. He was not frantic or compulsive in his service, but <u>intentional</u> and <u>focused</u>. *Word Picture*

Jesus didn't scurry around trying to meet every need. In fact, Mark 1:36–38 describes an incident when <u>he said no to needs</u> his disciples brought to him. In the next chapter, I will discuss resilience in ministry, which comes at least in part from <u>doing what we are called to do and nothing more</u>. Most people experience God's guidance most clearly while they are engaged in spiritual practices. Resilience in ministry is also enhanced when we serve from a foundation of knowing we are loved.

We Are Beloved

IMPT

We engage in spiritual practices because we are loved by God, not because we want to earn God's approval or to get God to do our bidding. As we experience that love, we are drawn closer to God. In *The Life of the Beloved*, Henri Nouwen writes,

> Every time you listen with great attentiveness to the voice that calls you the Beloved, you will discover within yourself a desire to hear that voice longer and more deeply. It is like discovering a well in the desert. Once you have touched wet ground, you want to dig deeper.[11]

The joy of feeling beloved is like water in the desert. We taste it and touch it, and we want more. Spiritual practices—many ways of engaging with the Bible, many ways of praying, and many other practices like attending church, small groups, Sabbath keeping, fasting, journaling, and hospitality—are ways that we act on our desire for more of God's presence.

Nouwen continues,

> The word "digging" might not be the best word since it suggests hard and painful work that finally leads me to the place where I can quench my thirst. Perhaps all we need to do is remove the dry sand that covers the well. There may be quite a pile of dry sand in our lives, but the One who so desires to quench our thirst will help us to remove it.[12]

Spiritual practices help us return to the well over and over. They help us remove the dry sand. And, as Nouwen points out, we don't engage in spiritual practices without help from "the One who so desires to quench our thirst." In fact, God empowers us to draw near. We engage in spiritual practices in the company of the God who loves us and calls us to draw near, empowering us to do so. This perspective on spiritual practices is essential.

A grace

Often, pastoral carers experience a powerful drive to rescue people from their pain, sorrow, and difficult situations. Because of the enormous challenges people face and our finite ability to respond, pastoral carers sometimes experience feelings of acute powerlessness. The living water from God's well is essential for us as carers to live with the not-knowing, not-curing, and not-healing that are major aspects of pastoral care in our complex and broken world. God's living water is also vital for us as we strive to be people who come alongside others without attempting to rescue them. Only God can rescue.

The living water from God's well is also essential for care recipients. Sometimes they have no desire to talk about God and God's presence with them, but we know God is already there, and we can rest in the security that God is with us as we listen and care. Sometimes care recipients are hungry to encounter God afresh through prayer, Bible reading, and other practices. In almost all instances, gentle questions about prayer and other spiritual practices can lead to fruitful conversations.

God's presence and God's transformation are essential themes of pastoral care that we embrace and augment with spiritual practices. God guides us, empowers us, transforms us, pours out love upon us, and invites us to draw near.

For Reflection and Discussion

1 Think of times in caring situations when you have felt comfortable and uncomfortable praying with a care recipient. What contributed to the comfort and discomfort?

2 Would you feel confident choosing and reading a passage from the Bible with a care recipient? Why or why not? What might help you feel more confident?

3 Which spiritual practices have you discussed or could you imagine discussing with a care recipient? In what ways would you like to grow in this area?

4 When you think of your own spiritual practices, what brings you joy? What makes you sad? Write a prayer for yourself related to your spiritual practices.

Resources

Calhoun, Adele Ahlberg. *Spiritual Disciplines Handbook*. Downers Grove, IL: InterVarsity, 2005.

> Presents more than sixty specific spiritual practices, with practical ideas for implementation along with purposes and Scriptures for each practice. A helpful resource to keep on hand to generate ideas and access descriptions of various practices.

Jones, Tony. *The Sacred Way: Spiritual Practices for Everyday Life*. Grand Rapids: Zondervan, 2005.

> Jones discusses sixteen spiritual practices, divided into two categories: contemplative approaches to spirituality and bodily approaches to spirituality. He compares spiritual practices to learning to play a sport or a musical instrument.

Baab, Lynne M. *Joy Together: Spiritual Disciplines for Your Congregation*. Louisville: Westminster John Knox, 2012.

> My book on communal spiritual practices gives many examples and stories of engaging in spiritual practices with others. It provides models and practical examples that carers may find helpful.

11
Resilience

IN 2003 I wrote a book on burnout among congregational volunteers. The title, *Beating Burnout in Congregations*, gave gentle homage to one of the books that influenced me the most as I wrote: *Beating Burnout* by Frank Minirth and four other authors.[1] Another book that I found extremely valuable was *Ministry Burnout* by John Sanford.[2]

Note that all three books I just mentioned have something in common, the use of the word "burnout" in the title. As I pondered a title for this chapter, I decided not to use that term. Instead, I'm using 〈"resilience," which communicates something about health and joy in serving.〉

I have a clear reason for focusing this chapter primarily on resilience rather than on burnout. In the decade and a half since I interviewed dozens of congregational leaders and members about burnout and wrote my book, a great deal of new research on the brain has helped us understand the significance of the way we talk about things. What we emphasize matters.

When we talk about what we don't want, even when we are saying we don't want it, we reinforce the brain pathways that nurture that belief, practice, or situation. When we talk about what we do want, we create and nurture new pathways.[3] Therefore, in this chapter I will primarily write about resilience, sometimes also called resiliency, a key component of healthy pastoral care. As carers, we need to be aware of the thoughts and actions that help us stay resilient, and we need to consider the ways we can help care recipients grow in resilience.

What is resilience? In chemistry, resilience is the ability of a substance to bounce back and return to its original shape. When discussing substances, synonyms for resilience include elasticity, flexibility, pliancy, suppleness, and robustness. Applying these characteristics to humans, participants in one research study defined resilience as "the ability to recover from setbacks, adapt well to change, and keep going in the face of adversity."[4]

Resilience in pastoral care is a foundation for the joy and fruitfulness that all pastoral carers hope for in themselves as well as in others. Resilience helps carers bounce back from challenges and make wise choices about stewardship of energy and gifts. Resilience helps prevent burnout.

Many habits and ways of thinking nurture resilience. For me, the Sabbath has been the best teacher about the significance of the rhythms that nurture resilience. Observing the Sabbath has helped me embrace life-giving rhythms in many other areas of life, and it has helped me grow in thinking in new ways that nurture resilience as well.

Sabbath

Right around the turn of the millennium, when I did the interviews for my book on burnout, the most common strategy for preventing burnout that my interviewees mentioned was keeping a Sabbath. I was quite surprised by this, because at that point my husband and I

> Resilient people possess thee characteristics—a staunch acceptance of reality; a deep belief, often buttressed by strongly held values, that life is meaningful; and an uncanny ability to improvise. You can bounce back from hardship with just one or two of these qualities, but you will only be truly resilient with all three.
>
> —Diane Coutu, *How Resilience Works*[5]

> Psychologically, rest contributes to resiliency, which is the capacity to return to well-being after a stressful situation. . . . Medically, rest is necessary for the body to recover from periods of work. During rest, the body removes toxins built up during exertion.
>
> —Claude J. Kayler, "Clergy Stress"[6]

had been observing a Sabbath for two decades, and we had talked with very few Christians about it.

Dave's and my Sabbath story began when we were young adults. We lived in Tel Aviv, Israel, for eighteen months. Dave taught in the dental school there, and I studied Hebrew full time for five months, then did volunteer work at our church until our first son was born. I expected that living in Israel would bring the Bible to life as we visited the sites of various stories, and that proved to be true. However, the biggest long-term gift Israel gave us was our experience of the Jewish Sabbath.

In our neighborhood, absolutely everything closed between sunset on Friday and sunset on Saturday: gas stations, mini-marts, supermarkets, shops, theaters, and restaurants. Three-quarters of the traffic went away. Sabbath days were so much quieter than weekdays and, at first, incredibly boring.

We didn't have a car, and the buses stopped running. For the first few months, I tried to arrange outings with friends at church who had cars. Then I got pregnant and began to feel pretty awful, so I was happy to stay around home.

Over many months, Dave and I finally settled into a Sabbath routine that not only worked for us but became a delight. We talked, prayed, walked, and ate leisurely meals together. Dave took his binoculars to the nearby empty lot and watched birds. I wrote long letters to family and friends. After our son was born, we continued the pattern, enjoying a relaxed day to be with our baby together.

When we returned to Seattle after our year and a half in Israel, we decided to continue to keep a Sabbath. Our friends at church were totally uninterested, so we quietly did it on our own. At that point, the Sabbath was simply not on the radar screen for Christians.

One friend actually told us it was wrong to keep a Sabbath as a Christian, arguing from Hebrews 4 that our Sabbath rest is fulfilled in Christ. That friend said that if we observed a Sabbath, we would be trying to earn God's approval through legalism. Dave and I talked about this friend's opinion, and we agreed that our friend completely misunderstood the essence of the Sabbath.

Like many Jews, we had experienced the Sabbath as a gift from God. Our day of stopping productive activity had become an opportunity to simply be a child of God one day each week, a day to rest in God's goodness and love, a day to remember God made and sustains the beautiful creation and the entire universe.

After arriving in Seattle, we changed our Sabbath day to Sundays. In the morning we went to church, and in the afternoon we tried to simply enjoy our son, and later our two sons. We went for walks, rode bicycles in parks, read to our kids, and invited friends over for dinner. We shut down consumer and work options like we had experienced in Israel, so we didn't shop or work on projects around the house.

We continued to observe a Sabbath as our children grew up, as I was ordained as a Presbyterian minister, and as I moved into a teaching career. Some of the details of our Sabbath observance have shifted with the years, but the practice remains. The Sabbath continues to be a gift.

The Sabbath as Teacher

non-cognitive impt

Stopping work and productivity, in a regular rhythm, has taught me deep truths in a noncognitive, experiential way. Keeping the Sabbath, more than anything else, has taught me about God's grace. It has also taught me that life is healthiest when lived in rhythms.

Stopping work and productivity, in a regular rhythm, has taught me deep truths in a noncognitive, experiential way.

Yes, God wants me to serve with energy and passion. I am valuable and necessary to God's work on earth. God wants to guide me into the right paths of service and empower me to follow those paths. And, yes, God wants me to stop working sometimes. God wants me to sit back and enjoy ease, comfort, and peace.

The Sabbath has impressed on my heart that God is God, and I am not. I am completely loved as a child of God before I do any act of service. All the goodness in my life comes to me as a free gift because of God's love for me.

Yes!

This perspective nurtures resilience in any kind of work or service. Knowing we are loved helps us show unconditional love to others, which is essential for pastoral carers. Stopping productive activities one day every week helps us experience that we are well-rounded people, free from compulsion to do one thing all the time. For pastoral carers, many of whom have a strong desire to serve whenever we see needs, the practice of stopping work every week can begin to build a habit of not being indispensable, a building block of resilience.

In addition to blessing us as carers, this is a healthy model for people *Yes* to whom we give care. As we strive to help care recipients find health and wholeness, sometimes the encouragement to stop trying to be productive every moment is exactly what people need to hear.

Rhythms in the Bible

In order to understand why keeping a Sabbath contributes so powerfully to resilience, an understanding of various perspectives on the nature of time is essential. In everyday life in Western countries today, time is often perceived as a frustrating commodity, a source of tension because there never seems to be enough of it. Time sometimes seems to go too slowly, especially when things are hard.

Usually, however, time seems to speed along, especially when we feel like our work just isn't fitting into the time allotted. In a 2010 study by the American Psychological Association about stress in

---

> The Sabbath has impressed on my heart that God is God, and I am not. I am completely loved as a child of God before I do any act of service. All the goodness in my life comes to me as a free gift because of God's love for me.

America, participants cited lack of time as the primary reason they had difficulty engaging in constructive behaviors to reduce their stress.[8]

The saying "time equals money" reveals the way we view time as a substance, almost a consumer item. At the same time, as Western culture has been increasingly influenced by Hinduism and Buddhism, a view of time as cyclical and repetitive has influenced many people, at least to some extent. This view of time, which some people experience as peaceful, can encourage a sense of resignation and purposelessness.

American/Western

← Eastern

Biblical

> We have value beyond what we produce or achieve. In fact, we are accepted by God before we do or achieve anything important.
>
> —Don Postema, *Catch Your Breath*[7]

The biblical view of time is quite different, with two perspectives held in tension. On the one hand, the Bible views time as moving forward toward a culmination that God will bring about, called the "Day of the Lord" in the Hebrew Scriptures. Jesus talks about many aspects of his return, including the admonition in four parables in Mathew 24:42–25:30 to stay awake and be ready for him to come back. This forward movement of time has purpose and a goal, and when we look back at history, we can see God's actions working toward God's purposes.

complementary: not competitive

However, time in the Bible is also rhythmical. The Jews had daily rhythms of prayer associated with rising, eating, and going to bed. They had a weekly rhythm marked by the Sabbath day. They also had a yearly rhythm of festivals when everyone stopped work. Because these rhythms are held in tension with the forward movement of time toward fulfillment of God's purposes, they are not part of a repetitive cycle. Instead, rhythms provide opportunities to remember God's faithfulness and goodness as God draws us forward.

|| liturgy

The Jewish year begins in the fall with Rosh Hashanah, the "head of the year" or New Years. In winter, Purim is a day to celebrate Esther's boldness and effective action to save the Jews. In spring, Passover encourages God's people to look back to the exodus. In early summer, the grain harvests are celebrated with the Feast of

Weeks, which is also linked to the giving of the law on Mount Sinai.

Right before Rosh Hashanah, the Feast of Tabernacles helps God's people remember the time in the wilderness after the exodus. The year ends with Yom Kippur, the Day of Atonement, a day of reflection and repentance for sin. All of these yearly rhythms point to God's acts in history and God's continued presence.

✓ For Jews in Jesus's time, life had built-in moments of stopping, usually in community with others. Those moments occurred during daily prayers, weekly Sabbath days, and yearly festivals. People lived in a communal rhythm of working and stopping work. The various components of the rhythm had different moods: thankfulness for meals, the peace of weekly rest, celebration at Passover, and sober self-assessment at the Day of Atonement. This sense of rhythm complemented the equally important flow of time toward the fulfillment of God's purposes.

Jesus modeled a life of rhythms, while looking ahead to God's consummation of history according to God's plan. Jesus went off alone in the mornings to spend time with the One he called Father, renewing Jesus's sense of commitment to his Father's purposes. He went to the synagogue on the Sabbath. He ate with his disciples. He modeled a life with rhythmical patterns that gave him the strength to continue his difficult ministry.

> *do we live in separation from that belief?*

Christians in the twenty-first century may have lost our confidence in the forward flow of history in fulfillment of God's purpose. We have definitely lost our sense of the rhythms of time, and that loss undermines resilience. Keeping the Sabbath is a foundational practice that restores a sense of life rhythms and helps us embrace other daily, weekly, monthly, and yearly patterns, because we learn to rely on God's grace more deeply and we learn how to stop compulsive activity.

Jesus modeled a life of rhythms, while looking ahead to God's consummation of history according to God's plan.

↓

> Doing religion workaholically is an assault on the very spirituality the church promises. How can you teach life more abundant when you are working yourself to death? No church hiring committee would consider giving a job to an applicant who was an active drug abuser. Why hire an active workaholic? Same disease, same consequences, same loss of spirituality.
>
> —Diane Fassel, *Working Ourselves to Death*[9]

Resilience and Rhythm

We are called to engage in rhythms for many reasons, and one of them involves our ability to bounce back when encountering challenges in pastoral care. Pastoral care definitely has joyful moments, where we are aware that our caring and service is bringing good fruit in the lives of care recipients. Pastoral carers rejoice in those moments. Resilience, however, is especially significant in the hard times, which are all too common.

Imagine that last month you and a group of others from your church helped an abused woman move out of her home. Yesterday she moved back in with her husband, even though nothing had changed in their relationship. How would you feel? How would you respond to what you feel?

Or perhaps yesterday you helped serve at a congregational dinner open to the wider community, and the power went out. You and a group of others washed dishes, pots, and pans by hand until midnight. Today you're exhausted.

Maybe you're coming to the end of a three-year commitment to chair the pastoral care team, and the administrative tasks have been much more challenging than you expected. You are deeply weary.

Effort ⟩ How can we nurture the resilience that helps us in the hard moments of service? Which rhythms help?

I once interviewed a presbytery executive, a man in his fifties who had served as a minister in several congregations and was now full of energy in his administrative role overseeing more than sixty Presbyterian congregations. He routinely worked fifty-hour weeks, and I never saw him display fatigue or discouragement. I asked him how he found energy for all the tasks he tackled, and he said he could work long weeks indefinitely as long as he had a weekly Sabbath day with his wife, including a long bike ride, plus a month off each year to go on longer bicycle trips with family members.

I also had a conversation with a quiet, sensitive minister in his forties who served a midsized congregation. He said he was able to deal with the needs of his parishioners for long periods of time, as well as his family at home, as long as each day had two building blocks: an hour of devotional time to read the Bible and pray, plus an hour of exercise. If he missed one of those, he would feel fatigue begin to creep in and he would lose his resilience.

Both of these men knew the key factors related to the rhythms of their lives that gave them resilience. Do you know the key factors *Figure these out!* for you? Are you comfortable talking about resilience with others, perhaps exploring the sources of robust energy for them?

Some of My Rhythms

In addition to my weekly Sabbath observance, I exercise three times a week, a pattern I have engaged in since I was in my twenties. When I exercise, my mind freewheels and somehow clears and empties itself. The exercise undoubtedly contributes to my physical health, but it also feels essential for my mental and emotional health.

When I was an associate minister serving a congregation in Seattle, my husband teased me about the numerous sources of support I gathered around me. He called it my support entourage, and in the midst of his teasing he expressed admiration that I knew the kinds of support I needed in order to serve well. Each month I actively sought out emotional and spiritual support by attending a clergywoman's support group, a support group with friends, and spiritual direction. Every month I got a massage.

In addition, the last Wednesday afternoon of each month I took several hours to walk a big circle on Seattle's Capitol Hill, visiting a restaurant and two beautiful churches. I prayed and reflected about my ministry, wrote in my journal, and set goals for the next month. The long walk, the silence in the two empty churches, and the journaling cleared my mind and also helped me think and pray more clearly. And the lunch in the restaurant, all by myself, felt luxurious, a sign that I am valuable and beloved apart from what I do.

My exercise pattern, weekly Sabbath, and the many monthly components of my "support entourage" helped me work hard. I had space to pray alone and with others, and to perceive God's guidance about what to do and not to do. I had time alone and with wise companions to think creatively about my ministry and my writing. I had time to reflect and time for social support. The many rhythms of my life helped me receive God's love as well as guidance for ministry and gave me resilience as each year of being a pastor seemed to involve a pile-up of added responsibilities and complexities.

Daily prayer times and weekly attendance at worship services are other components of the rhythmical pattern of life that I find essential. Others have talked to me about daily devotional times, weekly or biweekly attendance at small groups, meals with family members or housemates, prayer at bedtime with children or partners, consistent time spent doing hobbies, reading or writing a poem every morning, weekly walks with friends, and yearly retreats. These and many other rhythms nurture resilience.

Rhythmical aspects of life such as keeping the Sabbath, daily prayer and Bible study, weekly small groups, and weekly worship services can rightly be called spiritual practices. Repeated day after day or week after week, they impact our lives so much more profoundly than faith-related things we do occasionally without a pattern.

Be still and know that I am God!
I am exalted among the nations,
I am exalted in the earth.

—Psalm 46:10

Note: Not called "self care" b/c related to spirituality →

We are also influenced by rhythms that would probably not be described as spiritual practices. A habit of doing just about anything—including exercise, regular time with family and friends, time for crafts or music or poetry—creates a rhythm that can nurture resilience. I hope this chapter will encourage you to look at the rhythms of your life so you can grow in resilience. I'm also hoping that you'll talk about these rhythms with other pastoral carers.

Rhythms, Self-Care, and Balance

I have chosen to focus this chapter on rhythms, because the rhythm of the Sabbath has taught me so much. At various times in my life, I have found the concepts of balance and self-care to be equally helpful.

My favorite book on resilience for people in ministry is called *Clergy Self-Care: Finding a Balance for Effective Ministry* by longtime Alban Institute consultant Roy M. Oswald. Note that the title of the book uses both "self-care" and "balance."

Oswald makes a strong case for valuing self-care, and he gives many helpful suggestions for how to do it.[11] Even though he focuses on ordained ministers, many of my students who are lay chaplains or involved in other forms of lay ministry have found his ideas helpful.

In the early years of the 2000s, when I did quite a bit of speaking in churches on burnout, I was quite surprised when numerous Christians told me that neither "balance" nor "self-care" are

We must have some room to breathe. We need freedom to think and permission to heal. Our relationships are being starved to death by velocity. No one has the time to listen, let alone love. Our children lay wounded on the ground, run over by our high-speed good intentions. Is God now pro-exhaustion? Doesn't He lead people beside the still waters anymore? Who plundered those wide-open spaces of the past, and how can we get them back? There are no fallow lands for our emotions to lie down and rest in.

—Richard Swenson, *Margin*[10]

concepts affirmed in the Bible. The Bible, they said, emphasizes service and sacrifice, so we should not focus on caring for ourselves or on living a balanced life.

I would argue that the rhythms described and modeled in the Bible create a climate of self-care and balance without using those terms and without focusing on those goals. A pattern of consistently eating meals with loved ones, sharing food that someone cooked in a home, was accepted as a pattern of daily life in the Bible.

I can't tell you how many articles I've read in the health section of newspapers arguing that home-cooked food eaten with others nurtures well-being in so many ways, both physical and emotional. Saying a prayer together before each meal has the additional benefit of reminding everyone at the table that God is the giver of all sustenance and all good gifts.

Before electricity, a good night's sleep was accepted as normal and certainly not called "self-care." Before cars, people walked a lot and did many physical tasks every day without calling it "regular exercise." In Jesus's time, the weekly Sabbath and the yearly festivals provided abundant opportunities to stop, relax with others, do something besides work, and create balance in life.

Yes!

The stories in the Bible model a life based on communal rhythms, with many forms of social support built into daily life. The communal rhythms of life before electricity, cars, and fast food provided balance, enabled self-care, and created resilience. In this very different time, we need to consciously re-create the rhythms that will help us live healthy lives.

Thoughts and Beliefs

How we think about rhythms, self-care, and balance matters. In the first few years of the 2000s, around the time I wrote my book on burnout, I led several seminars around the country on stress, burnout, and the Myers-Briggs Type Indicator for the Center for

> Thus says the Lord:
> Stand at the crossroads, and look,
> and ask for the ancient paths,
> where the good way lies: and walk in it,
> and find rest for your souls.
>
> —Jeremiah 6:16

Applications of Psychological Type. I asked the participants about beliefs that lead to burnout.

The seminar participants had no trouble coming up with long lists of seductive but counterproductive beliefs such as:

- If I don't do it, it won't get done.
- No one can do it as well as I can.
- I can't be pleased with myself unless I'm exhausted.
- I have to be perfect.

good analogy about brain to cue reality

Most of the people generating the items on this list worked in business or counseling, but the statements are entirely relevant to caregivers. When we brainstormed those long lists of beliefs in the seminars, I felt profoundly tired. As I write those beliefs here in this chapter, I again feel tired. In contrast, when I wrote earlier about God's invitation into rhythms, I felt happy, grateful, and energized.

Participants in my seminars talked about the fact that these beliefs are deeply rooted and sometimes unconscious. Yet, these beliefs influenced them profoundly as they worked and served.

With my current interest in naming what I want my brain to develop, I've been working on a list of beliefs that foster resilience. In the area of rhythms, the list includes:

- God created me for rhythms.
- Rhythms in my life make me healthy and able to serve better.
- Sabbath rest is a gift God wants to give to me.
- When I'm tired, my body is giving me a message I need to pay attention to.

Nurturing a belief that humans are created for rhythms can help us commit to healthy habits. Pondering the rhythms of our lives helps us think creatively about patterns and habits, and the notion of rhythm removes the conviction—or compulsion—that we are supposed to do one thing all the time.

> People can use the process of doing church to dull their inner pain. We do well to ask ourselves from time to time: Am I willing to examine my Christian life and service for signs of being driven by unacknowledged neediness—rather than being called and led by God? For example, is my church life lived at a workaholic pace? If so, why? What need or whose need is this meeting? . . . Do I put so much effort into pastoral care because of an overwhelming need to be needed? Do I only sense God's love when I'm helping others?
>
> —Pamela Evans, *The Overcommitted Christian*[12]

Many carers are profoundly influenced by deep-rooted beliefs about service and sacrifice. Some of those beliefs may drive us to serve long past the appropriate time to stop. Some of those beliefs make it hard to bounce back from obstacles.

The kind-heartedness that motivates many pastoral carers can also drive us to provide care long after our energy is depleted. Maybe we continue to provide help when we are physically exhausted. Maybe we stay with someone in need long after the conversation has ceased to be productive. Sometimes other people's needs simply seem more real than our own.

Resilience, the ability to weather challenges, is essential for caregivers who want to serve long-term with joy. Resilience requires growing in the ability to balance our own needs with the needs of others.

Freedom and Joy in Serving

In the seminars I led about burnout and stress, the participants frequently talked about various forms of feeling indispensable and being unable to stop functioning. "If I don't do it, it won't get done right." In pastoral care, a parallel might be, "This person needs me, and who am I to think about my needs when this person's need is so great?"

My friend John was raised by a very anxious mother whose biggest concern was always, "What will the neighbors say?" John grew up to struggle with anxiety as well, and he bumped up against his anxiety when he served on a pastoral care team at church and later when he served in a ministry with international students.

One of John's biggest challenges in the area of resilience has been to let go of concerns about what others will think of him if he says "no" to a request for help or stops serving in order to watch a movie, get some exercise, or just rest for a while.

John has grown a lot in letting go of concerns about what others will think of him when he stops or slows down. Numerous things have helped him grow in this area: counseling, journaling, reading the Bible on his own and studying it with others in a men's group, and conversations with others who compulsively strive to look good to others.

Pastoral care teams provide opportunities to talk about the counterproductive beliefs that can drive carers to serve too long. Praying with other team members helps carers relinquish concerns into God's hands and enables carers to ask for God's guidance.

Teams provide settings for discussing the beliefs that nurture resilience, such as:

- Teams are valuable because team members share the load.
- God provides enough people and resources to get the job done.
- Sometimes saying "no" makes space for someone else to serve.
- Jesus praised Mary for sitting at his feet, even when Martha asked her to help with tasks (Luke 10:38–42).

Teams also provide opportunities for brainstorming about referring care recipients to other resources. Being prepared to refer care recipients to people in other caring professions and to other resources requires keeping lists of professionals, groups, classes, books, and websites. Keeping a list of resources fulfills two functions: we have resources available when others need them, and the list reminds us not to take on too much responsibility for others' situations.

> Resilience, the ability to weather challenges, is essential for caregivers who want to serve long-term with joy. Resilience requires growing in the ability to balance our own needs with the needs of others.

Sometimes that referral is required by law. Countries and states have different legal requirements for reporting and referring in cases of child abuse, suicide risk, and other serious situations. Pastoral carers, especially those in paid positions, need to be aware of the legal requirements in their setting.

Responsibility in Pastoral Care

When I look back on my seven years as an associate pastor in a Seattle congregation, I feel like I did a reasonably good job in many of the multitude of tasks a minister does. I also did a good job with habits that nurture resilience. My one big regret relates to an aspect of pastoral care. I can see now, looking back, that I took too much ownership of people's problems. I felt that I was responsible for fixing them or at least for helping in some significant way.

← Me too!

With each passing year in that congregation, I knew more of the personal stories of individuals. Their pain, suffering, and struggles weighed on me. By the time I left that congregation to pursue a PhD so I could go into teaching, I felt a sense of heaviness in every Sunday worship service as I looked around. When I saw individuals with whom I had had pastoral care conversations, I felt a small

Yes – I remember faces now!

Pastoral carers always need to be aware of needs that could better be met by someone else. Carers may want to refer care recipients to these or other resources:

- Counselors who specialize in various issues: marriage, addiction, trauma, and other specific needs
- AA and other forms of addiction treatment
- Healing prayer teams
- Stephen ministers or other trained lay pastoral carers
- Pastors, spiritual directors, or others who can help with prayer practices
- Small groups
- Parenting classes
- Classes on money management
- Anger management groups

measure of the pain they were carrying, and to some extent I felt like a failure because they were still struggling.

I wish I had known then how to feel sadness for others without feeling responsible. My excess of responsibility undermined my resilience in a way that still makes me grieve when I think about it.

Yes!

In recent years I've learned more about simply feeling my feelings, without making inner judgments about the situations that contributed to them and without judging myself for feeling them. I try to take feelings seriously, while also affirming that feelings come and go like weather.

I told my story of sixteen years of depression in the introductory chapter of this book for several reasons. I wanted readers to get to know me a little. I wanted to lay out the variety of forms of pastoral care I received from so many people and groups. I also wanted to point out that pastoral care can bring hope without fixing a problem.

Reflecting back on my experience as a person with depression and then as minister has helped me generate a list of beliefs I wish I had articulated earlier. These beliefs may help other carers to take enough responsibility, but not too much:

Student lists as last journal entry

- God is responsible for other people's lives. I help people by caring, but I am not ultimately responsible.
- I come alongside people in their pain, and I feel pain with them, but their pain belongs to God, not to me.
- God will help me know what to do and what not to do.
- Jesus's yoke is easy and his burden is light (Matt 11:28–30). I must take on Jesus's yoke and nothing more.

> For thus says the Lord God, the Holy One of Israel:
> In returning and rest you shall be saved;
> in quietness and in trust shall be your strength.
>
> —Isaiah 30:15

Rhythms Make Space

Rhythms nurture resilience because they keep us from getting stuck in one way of being or one activity. They help us believe deep inside that God calls us to both service and rest, work and play, exertion and relaxation, giving and receiving, mental and physical activity, and time alone and time with others. We are created for a variety of activities in many settings, and that variety undergirds resilience.

Rhythmical patterns of living enable balance and self-care. They also enhance creativity. A Sabbath day, exercise, time relaxing with people we love, and other rhythms make space to help us access the creative parts of our brain. Rhythms help us hear God's voice more clearly because we have space to listen.

Recently, in a conversation with a student about his service at church and his studies, he mentioned his desire to let God guide him into the right balance of studying and serving. He said, "Helping out at church is always a good thing to do, but it may not be the right thing to do."

In pastoral care, so many ways of helping can be good things to do but not necessarily the best way to give help that empowers. We need habits, practices, and life patterns that give us the time and space to reflect and hear God's voice about the very best ways to provide help.

In addition to making space for hearing God and allowing creative solutions to emerge, the rhythms described in this chapter help

Training Tips

If you lead training sessions for pastoral carers, you will probably want to

1. Give participants the opportunity to explore the influences in their lives that push them toward over-functioning and discuss ways they have experienced growth and healing in that area.

2. Give ample time to discuss rhythms that nurture health and well-being, as well as ways to nurture those rhythms.

3. Create a list of resources for referrals.

4. Provide information about the legal requirements for notifying authorities about suicide, sexual abuse, threats to children and vulnerable adults, and other situations in your location.

address the compulsion to serve that many Christians—particularly those with gifts and abilities in pastoral care—deal with. Keeping a Sabbath, repeated week after week and year after year, teaches us to rest in a rhythmical pattern: daily, weekly, monthly, and yearly.

The Sabbath helps Christians accept the reality that God is God and we are not. We don't have control over other people. Their problems belong to God, not us. We walk alongside, sharing the load as we journey together, growing in resilience as carers, as we help care recipients grow in resilience as well.

As you serve in pastoral care, I wish for you the resilience that leads to joy and fruitfulness in serving.

For Reflection and Discussion

1 Which of these concepts works best for you as you ponder the patterns of your life that nurture resilience: rhythms of life, self-care, or balance? Why? What do the three terms mean to you?

2 List the habits and rhythms that undergird resilience for you. Ponder how to amplify and nurture those habits. What new rhythms would you like to consider adopting?

3 Go back through the chapter and look at the bullet-pointed lists of beliefs and values that nurture resilience. Ponder the lists and evaluate which of the beliefs are easiest and hardest for you to embrace. Which beliefs would you like to affirm? What other beliefs already contribute to resilience for you or might do so?

4 Write a prayer for yourself in the area of resilience, asking for God's help to develop and nurture habits that undergird resilience.

Resources

Baab, Lynne M. *Sabbath Keeping: Finding Freedom in the Rhythms of Rest*. Downers Grove, IL: InterVarsity, 2005.

My book on the Sabbath tells the story of my husband's and my time in Israel and how our experience there shaped our Sabbath practice. It also includes stories from many other Sabbath keepers and reflection on biblical passages about the Sabbath.

Baab, Lynne M. "My New Spiritual Practice: Separating Thoughts from Feelings." *Lynne Baab* (blog), May 4, 2017. https://tinyurl.com /y8jj337c.

I wrote five consecutive blog posts about what I've learned about separating thoughts from feelings, how to feel the feelings and let go of thoughts that are not productive. I deeply wish I had known about these practices when I was a minister.

Swenson, Richard A. *Margin: Restoring Emotional, Physical, Financial, and Time Reserves to Overloaded Lives*. Colorado Springs: NavPress, 1992.

Swenson uses the word "margin" to describe the space between ourselves and our limits, a useful word that helps the reader explore sources of compulsive activity and how to think differently about the significance of stopping.

12

Pastoral Care and Hope

AN UNUSUAL pastoral care story began more than fifteen years ago, when a congregation in a historically African American neighborhood made a commitment to pay attention to the needs in the neighborhood and try to meet them. The staff and leaders of the church prayed consistently for God's guidance to perceive the community's needs.

One of the first observations they made was that in their low-income neighborhood, life expectancy was lower than their city's average and chronic disease was higher. Two men in the congregation who had been professional athletes noticed something else. The neighborhood offered no place to exercise.

To meet the need for a place to exercise and to help address the chronic health issues in the community, the congregation opened a small gym in a garage. Within two years, the membership was high enough to move to a larger portable building. Six years later the gym moved to its current location, a large space on the ground floor of a building dedicated to low-income housing.

The gym serves anyone in the community, and many of its members have no idea that the gym was the brainchild of a church. The gym has a few paid staff and many volunteer staff, who try to be warm and friendly with everyone who comes in. Both paid and volunteer staff are committed to pray for everyone who comes into the gym, asking for God's guidance about how to meet their needs.

Ronald, the current manager of the gym, reflects, "Our goal is to bless people with what we've been given, the opportunity to help people exercise. No one feels it's a Christian gym. Maybe later people will come to realize they've been served by a Christian, and they will gain a new perspective on Christianity, that Christians are honest and humble."

Anna, the director of the gym and a trainer, notes, "Our job is to serve people and show how good God is. Only God can convert people. That's the work of the Holy Spirit."

The neighborhood has changed a lot in the fifteen years since the congregation started paying attention to needs. Parts of it have gentrified, so both high- and low-income people frequent the gym. A large influx of Muslim refugees from East Africa began moving into the neighborhood about a decade ago.

As the congregation members got to know some of the migrants from East Africa, they learned that many of the women were experiencing weight gain in the United States. The food is different and daily life involves much less walking.

> For you, O Lord, are my hope, my trust, O Lord from my youth.
> Upon you I have leaned from my birth.
>
> —Psalm 71:5–6

Muslim women cannot exercise in the presence of men, so the gym offers classes four times a week for women only. The classes are offered in a large exercise room with the blinds pulled down over the windows. At the time of the classes, men are free to use the cardio and weight machines in the other part of the gym, but they are not admitted into the exercise room.

Anna says, "We saw exercise as a mode to tear down barriers—religion, background, culture. Sport breaks down barriers, and we have seen reconciliation happen over exercise when people share a common goal and passion." Anna says that online feedback calls it "the friendly gym," and she's happy that she and the other staff and volunteers have been able to create a nonintimidating environment and communicate a strong welcome.

Because much of the staffing of the gym comes from volunteers, the gym is able to offer a sliding scale for membership based on income. The church subsidized the gym for the first few years, but recently it has become self-sustaining.

Many of the themes in this book are illustrated by the gym. Pastoral carers today

- serve people inside and outside of congregations by listening to their needs;
- consider the particular needs of different ethnic groups;
- view people as holistic beings whose physical, emotional, relational, and spiritual health is closely intertwined;
- build relationships in the wider community so resources can be shared;
- try to empower people and help them find their own strength; and
- work collegially with others.

Consider again the list of seven verbs that describe pastoral care, quoted often in the first half of this book: healing, sustaining, guiding, reconciling, nurturing, liberating, and empowering. I can see components of each of those verbs in the ministry of this gym.

Pastoral care in our time can involve a big project, like a gym, and carers can find their place for service in the context of that larger ministry. Pastoral care can also involve an informal conversation, such as the one described in a blog post by Quaker pastor Philip Gulley. He writes about why he does not get discouraged. Despite all the awful things going on in the world, he sees people caring for each other in so many wonderful ways, and that care gives him hope.

He gives this example:

I was at a restaurant this week and noticed a waitress talking with a woman who was sitting by herself. The woman was facing me from across the room and I could [see] she was upset. She was crying. I watched as the waitress took the woman by the hand and stood beside her, listening, as the woman talked. The waitress was rubbing the woman's hand. She stood with that woman the longest time. The meals were stacking up, drinks needed refilled, the tables needed cleared, but no one raised their hand or called out to the waitress. Everyone just waited, patiently. Eventually the woman stopped crying, the waitress hugged her, and the rest of us sat there marveling.[1]

People caring for people is one of the most beautiful sights in the world, bringing hope in this world of too much darkness.

The kind of pastoral care ministry described in this book is profoundly hopeful for care recipients, because they can find their own strength in community with others. Their specific needs are considered, including their ethnic origins, past experiences, relationships, and longings. They receive love.

Pastoral care today is often provided by teams who support each other, pray together, brainstorm solutions to people's needs, and discuss helpful strategies to nurture resilience. In these settings, pastoral carers experience hope because we are reminded we don't have do all the work ourselves, and we can grow in our faith and in our skills. We also get to experience the joy of seeing care recipients growing in the direction of who they were meant to be, while we as caregivers grow as well.

New Testament scholar Joel Green describes the kind of caring that I have been advocating throughout this book:

"Caregiving" is in fact "caring" when it empowers and frees care receivers to fulfil their divine vocation as members of the human family. "Caregiving" in this sense does not arise from any interest in controlling the attitudes or behaviours of others, or predetermining the consequences of those actions, nor primarily from a sense of obligation. Caregiving that takes its bearings from the character of God expressed in creation grows out of one's own interested love and concern for human wholeness.[2]

I am in awe of the people featured in the many stories I have recounted in this book. So many Christians are trying to care for others in ways that come from deep love and passionate concern for human wholeness. I am so grateful God has called them to do the many forms of pastoral care that they engage in. I couldn't do so many of the ministries I have described. I thank God for the diversity of gifts in the body of Christ, and the variety of passions and energy within the Christian community that make possible so many forms of caring.

The prayer in Ephesians 3 touches on some of the themes I've written about, including God's gift of hope, God's call to service rooted and grounded in love, and God's empowerment of both carers and care recipients. I am praying this prayer for all who

Training Tips

If you offer training for caregivers,

1 Go back to the table of contents of this book and look at it with the training group. Ask participants to discuss the parts of the book they learned the most from and that they were most surprised by.

2 Consider together the seven trends discussed in the first half of the book. Brainstorm ideas for further exploration of two or three of the trends that are most relevant in your context.

3 Be sure to give participants the opportunity to reflect on the four skills discussed in the second half of the book. Brainstorm ways to get more training in each of the four skill areas.

4 Help participants set goals for further growth and development.

read this book. May all of us strive to grow as Christian pastoral caregivers who rely on God's strength and want to convey God's love.

> I pray that the God of our Lord Jesus Christ, the Father of glory, may give you a spirit of wisdom and revelation as you come to know him, so that, with the eyes of your heart enlightened, you may know what is the hope to which he has called you, what are the riches of his glorious inheritance among the saints, and what is the immeasurable greatness of his power for us who believe, according to the working of his great power. (Eph 1:17–19)

For Reflection and Discussion

1 Looking back over this book, which components of pastoral care today surprised you the most? How would your own patterns of caring change if you incorporated insights from those new trends?

2 Looking back over the four chapters on pastoral care skills, which chapter surprised you the most by its inclusion or by what was covered? Why? What might your surprise teach you?

3 If someone asked you what the connection is between pastoral care and hope, how would you respond?

4 Write a prayer for yourself as a Christian pastoral carer, incorporating two or three of the major insights you gained from this book.

Notes

Introduction: Christian Pastoral Care in the Twenty-First Century

1. Nancy Tatom Ammerman, *Sacred Stories, Spiritual Tribes: Finding Religion in Everyday Life* (New York: Oxford University Press, 2013).
2. I heard Ammerman talk about her research in her two keynote addresses on June 29 and July 1, 2013, at the Australia New Zealand Association for Theological Schools annual conference, held at Laidlaw College in Auckland.
3. Ammerman, keynote address.
4. Ammerman, keynote address.
5. Wayne E. Oates, *Grief, Transition, and Loss: A Pastor's Practical Guide* (Minneapolis: Fortress Press, 1997), 14.
6. Ammerman, keynote address.
7. Eugene H. Peterson, "Curing Souls: The Forgotten Art," *Christianity Today*, Summer 1983, https://tinyurl.com/ybckrpeq.
8. Peterson, "Curing Souls."
9. Peterson, "Curing Souls."
10. Peterson, "Curing Souls."

Chapter 1: Pastoral Care Has Many Models

1. The Alpha Marriage Course, http://www.themarriagecourses.org.
2. William A. Clebsch and Charles R. Jaekle, *Pastoral Care in Historical Perspective* (New York: Harper & Row, 1967), 4.
3. Emmanuel Y. Lartey, *In Living Color: An Intercultural Approach to Pastoral Care and Counseling* (London: Jessica Kingsley, 2003), 62.
4. Stephen Pattison, *A Critique of Pastoral Care* (London: SCM, 2000), 12.
5. Eugene Peterson, "Curing Souls: The Forgotten Art," *Christianity Today*, Summer 1983, https://tinyurl.com/ybckrpeq.
6. Pattison, *Critique of Pastoral Care*, 13.

7. Alistair V. Campbell, *Professionalism and Pastoral Care*, ed. Don S. Browning (Philadelphia: Fortress Press, 1985), 11.

8. Barbara J. McClure, *Moving beyond Individualism in Pastoral Care and Counseling: Reflections on Theory, Theology and Practice* (Cambridge: Lutterworth, 2011), 20.

9. "Rev. Seward Hiltner, 74, Dies; Taught at Princeton Seminary," *New York Times*, November 28, 1984, https://tinyurl.com/y9y6e6ob.

10. Seward Hiltner, *Pastoral Counseling* (New York: Abingdon-Cokesbury, 1949), cited in Gaylord B. Noyce, "Has Ministry's Nerve Been Cut by the Pastoral Counseling Movement?" *Christian Century*, February 1, 1978, 104.

11. Bonnie J. Miller-McLemore, "The Human Web: Reflections on the State of Pastoral Theology," *Christian Century*, April 7, 1993, 366.

12. Miller-McLemore, "Human Web," 366.

13. Charles Gerkin, *An Introduction to Pastoral Care* (Nashville: Abingdon, 1997), 88.

14. Henri Nouwen, "Care," *Cornerstone* 26, no. 11 (1997): 8.

15. Nouwen, "Care," 8.

16. Nouwen, "Care," 8.

Chapter 2: Teams and a Variety of Individuals Provide Pastoral Care

1. Howard W. Stone, *Theological Context for Pastoral Caregiving: Word in Deed* (London: Routledge, 1996), 13.

2. Stephen Ministries, http://www.stephenministries.org/.

3. Peggy Way, *Created by God: Pastoral Care for All God's People* (St. Louis, MO: Chalice, 2005), 3.

4. Tim Farabaugh, *Lay Pastoral Care Giving* (Nashville: Discipleship Resources, 2009), 14.

5. Farabaugh, *Lay Pastoral Care Giving*, 14.

6. Farabaugh, *Lay Pastoral Care Giving*, 15.

7. Howard W. Stone, "The Congregational Setting of Pastoral Counseling: A Study of Pastoral Counseling Theorists from 1949–1999," *Journal of Pastoral Care* 55, no. 2 (2001): 181–96.

8. Farabaugh, *Lay Pastoral Care Giving*, 15.

9. Gene Fowler, "The Ministry of Pastoral Care in Twenty-First-Century Protestant Congregations," *Pastoral Psychology* 61, no. 2 (2012): 198.

10. Fowler, "Ministry of Pastoral Care," 200.

11. Frederick Buechner, *Wishful Thinking: A Seeker's ABC* (San Francisco: HarperSanFrancisco, 1993), 119.

Chapter 3: Christian Pastoral Care Is Grounded in the Triune God

1. Allan Hugh Cole, "What Makes Care Pastoral?" *Pastoral Psychology* 59, no. 6 (2010): 719.

2. Henry G. Covert, *Ministry to the Incarcerated* (Chicago: Loyola University Press, 1995), 82–83. In the original, each item on the list has comments and biblical citations.

3. Covert, *Ministry to the Incarcerated*, 80.

4. Covert, *Ministry to the Incarcerated*, 72–74.

5. Covert, *Ministry to the Incarcerated*, 80.

6. Covert, *Ministry to the Incarcerated*, 86.

7. Stephen Pattison, *A Critique of Pastoral Care* (London: SCM, 2000), 9.

8. Neil Holm, "Toward a Theology of the Ministry of Presence in Chaplaincy," *Journal of Christian Education* 52, no. 1 (May 2009): 15. This article is readily available online in PDF form.

9. Holm, "Toward a Theology," 16.

10. Among many books I could cite, I'll mention two books by Stanley J. Grenz because the titles capture the wording used so often by theologians in recent decades: *Created for Community: Connecting Christian Belief with Christian Living* (Wheaton, IL: Victor Books, 1996), and *The Social God and the Relational Self: A Trinitarian Theology of the Imago Dei* (Louisville: Westminster John Knox, 2001).

11. Tim Farabaugh, *Lay Pastoral Care Giving* (Nashville: Discipleship Resources, 2009), 14.

Chapter 4: Christian Pastoral Care Is Missional

1. Wendy Bailey, "You Go Nowhere by Accident," *The Story* (blog), September 30, 2013, https://tinyurl.com/y9p48h44.

2. Alan Hirsch, "Defining Missional," *Christianity Today*, Fall 2008, https://tinyurl.com/yct3z8lc.

3. Hirsch, "Defining Missional."

4. Graham Hill, *Salt, Light, and a City: Introducing Missional Ecclesiology* (Eugene, OR: Wipf & Stock, 2012), 267.

5. Alan Roxburgh and Fred Romanuk, *The Missional Leader: Equipping Your Church to Meet a Changing World* (San Francisco: Jossey-Bass, 2006), 17.

6. Kim Hammond and Darren Cronshaw, *Sentness: Six Postures of Missional Christians* (Downers Grove, IL: InterVarsity, 2014).

7. Alan Roxburgh, *Joining God, Remaking the Church, Changing the World: The New Shape of the Church in Our Time* (New York: Morehouse, 2015), 18.

Chapter 5: Pastoral Care Occurs across Ethnicities and Religions

1. For example, Brenda Salter McNeil and Rick Richardson, *The Heart of Racial Justice* (Downers Grove, IL: InterVarsity, 2004), 161–63; and Carl Zimmer, "Genes for Skin Color Rebut Dated Notions of Race, Researchers Say," *New York Times*, October 12, 2017, https://tinyurl.com/y9ns8zb6.

2. Stephen A. Rhodes, *Where the Nations Meet: The Church in a Multicultural World* (Downers Grove, IL: InterVarsity, 1998), 111.

3. Rhodes, *Where the Nations Meet*, 110.

4. David Pearson, "Crossing Ethnic Thresholds: Multiculturalisms in Comparative Perspective," in *Nga Patai: Racism and Ethnic Relations in Aotearoa New Zealand*, ed. Paul Spoonley, David Pearson, and Cluny Macpherson (Palmerston North, NZ: Dunmore, 1996), 248.

5. Jonathan Chaplin, *Multiculturalism: A Christian Retrieval* (London: Theos, 2011), 32.

6. Daniel G. Groody, "Theology in the Age of Migration: Seeing the Image of Christ in the Eyes of a Stranger," *National Catholic Reporter*, September 14, 2009, https://tinyurl.com/y73eqyxk.

7. Charles van Engen, *Mission on the Way* (Grand Rapids: Baker, 1996), 179, quoted in Kevin R. Ward, *Losing Our Religion: Changing Patterns of Believing and Belonging in Secular Western Societies* (Eugene, OR: Wipf & Stock, 2013), 186.

8. OECD, "Foreign Born Population," https://tinyurl.com/y87b6ezf. The New Zealand figure comes from "2013 Census Quick Stats about Culture and Identity," Statistics New Zealand, April 15, 2014, https://tinyurl.com/y7yb2bat.

9. Peggy Levitt and B. Nada Jaworsky, "Transnational Migration: Past Developments and Future Trends," *Annual Review of Sociology* 33, no. 1 (2007): 131.

10. Soong-Chan Rah, *Many Colors: Cultural Intelligence for a Changing Church* (Chicago: Moody, 2010).

11. Elizabeth Conde-Frazier, S. Steve Hang, and Gary A. Parrett, eds., *A Many Colored Kingdom: Multicultural Dynamics for Spiritual Formation* (Grand Rapids: Baker, 2004).

12. Mark DeYmaz and Harry Li, *Ethnic Blends: Mixing Diversity into Your Local Church* (Grand Rapids: Zondervan, 2010).

13. For example, Diana L. Eck, "Is Our God Listening? Exclusivism, Inclusivism, and Pluralism," in *Islam and Global Dialogue: Religious Pluralism and the Pursuit of Peace*, ed. Roger Boase (Aldershot: Ashgate, 2005), 21–49; Andrew Wingate, "Mission as Dialogue: A Contextual Study from Leicester, UK," in *The Gospel among Religions: Christian Ministry, Theology, and Spirituality in a Multifaith World*, ed. David R. Brockman and Ruben L. F. Habito (Maryknoll, NY: Orbis, 2010), 153–67; David Burnett, *Clash of Worlds: What Christians Can Do in a World of Cultures in Conflict* (London: Monarch, 2002).

14. Daniel G. Groody, "Crossing the Divide: Foundations of a Theology of Migration," *Theological Studies* 70, no. 3 (2009): 638–67.

15. Katherine W. Phillips, "How Diversity Works," *Scientific American* 311, no. 4 (October 2014): 31.

16. Phillips, "How Diversity Works," 35.

17. For example, Brad Christerson and Michael Emerson, "The Costs of Diversity in Religious Organizations: An In-Depth Case Study," *Sociology of Religion* 64, no. 2 (2003): 163–81; "Report of the World Council of Churches Consultation on Mission and Ecclesiology of the Migrant Churches," *International Review of Missions* 100, no. 1 (April 2011): 104–7.

18. Paula Harris and Doug Schaupp, *Being White: Finding Our Place in a Multiethnic World* (Downers Grove, IL: InterVarsity, 2004), 93. In the original, each bullet point has a paragraph of text with it.

Chapter 6: Pastoral Care Empowers

1. Michael Hobbes, "America Already Has Extreme Vetting," *Rottin' in Denmark* (blog), February 15, 2017, https://tinyurl.com/ycudswos.

2. Book synopsis on Abe Books of *Help: The Original Human Dilemma* by Grant Keizer (San Francisco: HarperOne, 2004), https://tinyurl.com/yd24jsne.

3. Michael Hobbes, "Stop Trying to Save the World," *The New Republic*, November 17, 2014, https://tinyurl.com/hthj9zw.

4. Michael Hobbes discusses millennials' interest in outcomes research in several of his articles, including "How Mark Zuckerberg Should Give Away $45 Billion," *Huffington Post*, February 24, 2016, https://tinyurl.com/yax4z7hf.

5. Henri Nouwen, "Care," *Cornerstone* 26, no. 11 (1997): 8.

6. Peggy Way, *Created by God: Pastoral Care for All God's People* (St. Louis, MO: Chalice, 2005), 4.

7. Way, *Created by God*, 4.

8. Jeffrey W. Dwyer, Gary R. Lee, and Thomas B. Jankowski, "Reciprocity, Elder Satisfaction, and Caregiver Stress and Burden: The Exchange of Aid in the Family Caregiving Relationship," *Journal of Marriage and the Family* 56, no. 1 (February 1994): 36.

9. Christine Pohl, *Making Room: Recovering Hospitality as a Christian Tradition* (Grand Rapids: Eerdmans, 1999).

10. Amy G. Oden, *And You Welcomed Me: A Sourcebook on Hospitality in Early Christianity* (Nashville: Abingdon, 2001), 36.

11. Quoted in Christine D. Pohl, "A Community's Practice of Hospitality: The Interdependence of Practices and of Communities," in *Practicing Theology: Beliefs and Practices in Christian Life*, ed. Miroslav Volf and Dorothy C. Bass (Grand Rapids: Eerdmans, 2002), 134.

12. Howard Stone, *Theological Context for Pastoral Caregiving: Word in Deed* (London: Routledge, 1996), 13.

13. John Patton, *Pastoral Care: An Essential Guide* (Nashville: Abingdon, 2005), 31.

14. Eugene H. Peterson, "Curing Souls: The Forgotten Art," *Christianity Today*, Summer 1983, https://tinyurl.com/ybckrpeq.

15. Aart M. van Beek, "A Cross-Cultural Case for Convergence in Pastoral Thinking and Training," *Pastoral Psychology* 59, no. 4 (2010): 479.

Chapter 7: Pastoral Carers Consider the Web of Relationships

1. According to the 2013 Census, 15 percent of the New Zealand population is Māori and 7 percent were born in the Pacific Islands. These figures do not include second-generation migrants from the Pacific Islands, who are also communally oriented and who outnumber the first-generation migrants. "2013 Census Quick Stats about Māori," Statistics New Zealand, December 3, 2013, https://tinyurl.com/y9m5nqf3; Ministry of Pacific Island Affairs, "Demographic Fact Sheet," https://tinyurl.com/yddy6mgx.

2. Emmanuel Y. Lartey, "Global Views for Pastoral Care and Counseling: Postmodern, Post-Colonial, Post-Christian, Post-Human, Post-Pastoral" (address at the 7th Asia-Pacific Congress on Pastoral Care and Counseling, July 15, 2009, Perth, Australia).

3. Peggy Way, *Created by God: Pastoral Care for All God's People* (St. Louis, MO: Chalice, 2005), 1.

4. Way, *Created by God*, 2.

5. Martin Luther King Jr., "A Time to Break the Silence," quoted in Douglas A. Hicks and Mark R. Valeri, *Global Neighbors: Christian Faith and Moral Obligation in Today's Economy* (Grand Rapids: Eerdmans, 2008), 31.

6. Tony Kriz, "Blessings of a Post-Christian Culture," *Christianity Today*, March 2015, https://tinyurl.com/ybrtrgh8.

7. Kriz, "Blessings of a Post-Christian Culture."

8. Howard W. Stone, *Theological Context for Pastoral Caregiving: Word in Deed* (London: Routledge, 1996), 13.

9. Russell McLendon, "11 Alarming Facts about Sea Level Rise," Mother Nature Network, February 26, 2016, https://tinyurl.com/ybon3njx.

10. Daniel E. Forman, Aaron D. Berman, Carolyn H. McCabe, Donald S. Baim, and Jeanne Y. Wei, "PTCA in the Elderly: The 'Young-Old' versus the 'Old-Old,'" *Journal of the American Geriatrics Society* 40, no. 1 (1992): 19–22.

11. Pamela Cooper-White, *Shared Wisdom: Use of the Self in Pastoral Care and Counseling* (Minneapolis: Fortress Press, 2004), 125.

12. Cooper-White, *Shared Wisdom*, 125, italics in original.

13. Cooper-White, *Shared Wisdom*, 125–26.

Chapter 8: Old/New Sources of Stress

1. Barbara L. Carlozzi, Carrie Winterowd, R. Stephen Harrist, Nancy Thomason, Kristi Bratkovich, and Sheri Worth, "Spirituality, Anger, and Stress in Early Adolescence," *Journal of Religion and Health* 49, no. 4 (2010): 447.

2. Quoted in Joe D. Wilmoth and Samantha Smyser, "The ABC-X Model of Family Stress in the Book of Philippians," *Journal of Psychology and Theology* 37, no. 3 (2009): 155.

3. Thomas H. Holmes and Richard H. Rahe, "The Social Readjustment Rating Scale," *Journal of Psychosomatic Research* 11, no. 2 (1967): 213–18.

4. Jeanne L. Jensma, "Critical Incident Intervention with Missionaries," *Journal of Psychology and Theology* 27, no. 2 (1999): 131.

5. Two research studies that help to explain what was going on in my body are: Elissa S. Epel, Rachel Lapidus, Bruce McEwen, and Kelly Brownell, "Stress May Add Bite to Appetite in Women: A Laboratory Study of Stress-Induced Cortisol and Eating Behavior," *Psychoneuroendocrinology* 26, no. 1 (2001): 37–49; and Elissa S. Epel, Bruce McEwen, Teresa Seeman, et al., "Stress and Body Shape: Stress-Induced Cortisol Secretion Is Consistently Greater among Women with Central Fat," *Psychosomatic Medicine* 62, no. 5 (2000): 623–32.

6. One research article that explains this phenomenon is Robert C. Andrew, Olive Herlihy, Dawn E. W. Livingstone, Ruth Andrew, and Brian R. Walker, "Abnormal Cortisol Metabolism and Tissue Sensitivity to Cortisol in Patients with Glucose Intolerance," *Journal of Clinical Endocrinology and Metabolism* 87, no. 12 (2002): 5587–93.

7. Quoted by Sarah Klein in "6 Surprising Causes of Inflammation—And What You Can Do about It," *Prevention*, May 14 2015, https://tinyurl.com/yd6bn2vh.

8. Saul McLeod, "Stress and Life Events," *Simply Psychology*, 2010, https://tinyurl.com/ydavmca5.

9. Allen D. Kanner, James C. Coyne, Catherine Schaefer, and Richard S. Lazarus, "Comparison of Two Modes of Stress Measurement: Daily Hassles and Uplifts versus Major Life Events," *Journal of Behavioral Medicine* 4, no. 1 (1981): 1–39.

10. American Psychological Association, "Stress in America Findings," November 9, 2010, https://tinyurl.com/ybube9xs.

11. One example of a newer inventory measuring the effects of various stressors is described by Craig A. Jackson in "The Life Events Inventory (LEI)," *Occupational Medicine* 59, no. 3 (2009): 208.

12. Jana Kasperkevic, "Why Is America So Afraid to Take a Vacation?" *The Guardian*, September 7, 2015, https://tinyurl.com/yc5jxhzx.

13. See the sidebar in chapter 5 for additional countries. Percentages from OECD, "Foreign Born Population," https://tinyurl.com /y87b6ezf. The New Zealand figure comes from "2013 Census Quick Stats about Culture and Identity," Statistics New Zealand, April 15, 2014, https://tinyurl.com/y7yb2bat.

14. Quoted in Claude J. Kayler, "Clergy Stress: A Study of Stressors and Stress-Relieving Practices among United Methodist Clergy across Three Districts of the Western North Caroline Conference" (Doctor of Ministry Thesis, Asbury Theological Seminary, 2011), 68.

15. Reuben Hill, "Generic Features of Families Under Stress," *Social Casework* 49, no. 2 (1958): 141.

16. Joan M. Patterson, "Understanding Family Resilience," *Journal of Clinical Psychology* 58, no. 3 (2002): 236.

17. Karen D. Lincoln, Linda M. Chatters, and Robert Joseph Taylor, "Social Support, Traumatic Events, and Depressive Symptoms Among African Americans," *Journal of Marriage and Family* 67, no. 3 (2005): 754.

18. George R. Faller and Heather Wright, *Sacred Stress: A Radically Different Approach to Using Life's Challenges for Positive Change* (Woodstock, VT: Skylight Paths, 2016), 119.

19. Mariana Sanchez, Frank R. Dillon, Maritza Concha, and Mario De La Rosa, "The Impact of Religious Coping on the Acculturative Stress and Alcohol Use of Recent Latino Immigrants," *Journal of Religion and Health* 54, no. 6 (2015): 1988.

20. Faller and Wright, *Sacred Stress*, 123.

21. Faller and Wright, *Sacred Stress*. The items in this list are major themes throughout the book.

22. Faller and Wright, *Sacred Stress*, 117.

23. Fallen and Wright (*Sacred Stress*, 117) make the point that optimists have better outcomes when facing stress. They cite Valerie Maholmes, *Fostering Resilience and Well-Being in Children and Families in Poverty: Why Hope Still Matters* (Oxford: Oxford University Press, 2014), 14.

Chapter 9: Listening Skills

1. Dietrich Bonhoeffer, *Life Together* (London: SCM, 1967), 75.
2. Most of these minimal encouragers comes from Robert Bolton, "Listening Is More Than Merely Hearing," in *Bridges Not Walls: A Book about Interpersonal Communication*, ed. John Stewart (New York: McGraw-Hill, 1990), 186.
3. Bolton, "Listening," 188.
4. Richard Dimbleby and Graeme Burton, *More Than Words: An Introduction to Communication*, 4th ed. (London: Routledge, 2007), 88.
5. Bolton, "Listening," 188–89.
6. Bolton, "Listening," 189.
7. Craig Satterlee, "Holy and Active Listening," Alban Institute, https://tinyurl.com/y7n5tsxb. Adapted from *When God Speaks through Change: Preaching in Times of Congregational Transition* (Herndon, VA: Alban Institute, 2005).
8. Kathleen S. Verderber and Rudolph F. Verderber, *Inter-Act: Interpersonal Communication Concepts, Skills and Contexts*, 10th ed. (New York: Oxford University Press, 2004), 211.
9. Verderber and Verderber, *Inter-Act*, 214.
10. I encourage my chaplaincy and pastoral care students to watch "Brené Brown on Empathy" on YouTube (https://tinyurl.com/y8u3gvvg), which explains empathy well but contrasts it with a painfully paternalistic and negative view of sympathy.
11. The contrasts described in this section come from Joseph DeVito, Susan O'Rourke, and Linda O'Neill, *Human Communication*, New Zealand edition (Auckland: Longman, 2000), 68–72. The comments on each contrast are my own.
12. Bolton, "Listening," 183–84.
13. The first four ways to shut down listening are listed by Richard Bolstad and Margot Hamblett in *Transforming Communication* (Auckland: Longman, 1997), 88–89. I have amended their descriptions.
14. Henri Nouwen, "Care," *Cornerstone* 26, no. 11 (1997): 8.
15. Nouwen, "Care," 8.

Chapter 10: Spiritual Practices

1. Richard J. Foster, *A Celebration of Discipline* (San Francisco: Harper & Row, 1978). Foster also created a helpful workbook with

Kathryn A. Yanni entitled *Celebrating the Disciplines* (San Francisco: HarperSanFrancisco, 1992).

2. Henri Nouwen, "Moving from Solitude to Community to Ministry," *Leadership* 16, no. 2 (Spring 1995): 81.

3. Adele Ahlberg Calhoun, *Spiritual Disciplines Handbook* (Downers Grove, IL: InterVarsity, 2005), 17.

4. Calhoun, *Spiritual Disciplines Handbook*, 17.

5. Marjorie J. Thompson, *Soul Feast: An Invitation to the Christian Spiritual Life* (Louisville: Westminster John Knox, 1995), xv.

6. Thompson, *Soul Feast*, xv.

7. "Lord Jesus Christ, Son of God, have mercy on me, a sinner." This ancient prayer is based on the story of the Pharisee and the tax collector in Luke 18:9–14.

8. Andrew Purves, *Pastoral Theology in the Classical Tradition* (Louisville: Westminster John Knox, 2001), 118.

9. Purves, *Pastoral Theology*, 118.

10. Richard J. Foster and Gayle D. Beebe, *Longing for God: Seven Paths of Christian Devotion* (Downers Grove, IL: InterVarsity, 2009), 97.

11. Henri Nouwen, *Life of the Beloved* (New York: Crossroad, 1992), 31.

12. Nouwen, *Life of the Beloved*, 31–32.

Chapter 11: Resilience

1. Frank Minirth, Paul Meier, Don Hawkins, Chris Thurmon, and Rich Flournoy, *Beating Burnout: Balanced Living for Busy People* (New York: Inspirational Press, 1997). Combines two earlier books: *How to Beat Burnout* and *Before Burnout*.

2. John A. Sanford, *Ministry Burnout* (Louisville: Westminster John Knox, 1982).

3. Sharon Begley, science writer for the *Wall Street Journal*, describes research studies about the way our actions and thoughts impact our brain in *Train Your Mind, Change Your Brain: How a New Science Reveals Our Extraordinary Potential to Transform Ourselves* (New York: Ballantine, 2008).

4. Andrea Ovans, "What Resilience Means, and Why It Matters," *Harvard Business Review*, January 5, 2015, https://tinyurl.com/nf9zrcu.

5. Quoted in Ovans, "What Resilience Means."

6. Claude J. Kayler, "Clergy Stress: A Study of Stressors and Stress-Relieving Practices among United Methodist Clergy across Three Districts of the Western North Carolina Conference" (Doctor of Ministry Thesis, Asbury Theological Seminary, 2011), 45–46.

7. Don Postema, *Catch Your Breath: God's Invitation to Sabbath Rest* (Grand Rapids: CRC Press, 1997), 66.

8. American Psychological Association, "Stress in America Findings," November 9, 2010, https://tinyurl.com/ybube9xs.

9. Diane Fassel, *Working Ourselves to Death: The High Cost of Workaholism and the Rewards of Recovery* (Lincoln, NE: iUniverse, 2000), quoted in Pamela Evans, *The Overcommitted Christian: Serving God without Wearing Out* (Downers Grove, IL: InterVarsity, 2001), 46.

10. Richard A. Swenson, *Margin: Restoring Emotional, Physical, Financial, and Time Reserves to Overloaded Lives* (Colorado Springs: NavPress, 1992), 30.

11. Roy M. Oswald, *Clergy Self-Care: Finding a Balance for Effective Ministry* (Washington, DC: Alban Institute, 1991).

12. Pamela Evans, *The Overcommitted Christian: Serving God without Wearing Out* (Downers Grove, IL: InterVarsity, 2001), 40.

Chapter 12: Pastoral Care and Hope

1. Philip Gulley, "Why I Am a Progressive Christian," *Grace Talks* (blog), https://tinyurl.com/ycb2jwvs.

2. Joel B. Green, "Caring as Gift and Goal: Biblical and Theological Reflections," in *The Crisis of Care: Affirming and Restoring Caring Practices in the Helping Professions*, ed. Susan S. Phillips and Patricia Benner (Washington, DC: Georgetown University Press, 1994), 154.

Bibliography

American Psychological Association. "Stress in America Findings." November 9, 2010. https://tinyurl.com/ybube9xs.

Ammerman, Nancy Tatom. Keynote addresses given at the Australia New Zealand Association for Theological Schools Annual Conference, June 29 and July 1, 2013, Laidlaw College, Auckland, New Zealand.

———. *Sacred Stories, Spiritual Tribes: Finding Religion in Everyday Life*. New York: Oxford University Press, 2013.

Andrew, Robert C., Olive Herlihy, Dawn E. W. Livingstone, Ruth Andrew, and Brian R. Walker. "Abnormal Cortisol Metabolism and Tissue Sensitivity to Cortisol in Patients with Glucose Intolerance." *Journal of Clinical Endocrinology and Metabolism* 87, no. 12 (2002): 5587–93.

Baab, Lynne M. *Joy Together: Spiritual Disciplines for Your Congregation.* Louisville: Westminster John Knox, 2012.

———. "My New Spiritual Practice: Separating Thoughts from Feelings." *Lynne Baab* (blog), May 4, 2017. https://tinyurl.com /y8jj337c.

———. *The Power of Listening: Building Skills for Mission and Ministry.* Lanham, MD: Rowman & Littlefield, 2014.

———. *Sabbath Keeping: Finding Freedom in the Rhythms of Rest.* Downers Grove, IL: InterVarsity, 2005.

Bailey, Wendy. "You Go Nowhere by Accident." *The Story* (blog). September 30, 2013. https://tinyurl.com/y9p48h44.

Begley, Sharon. *Train Your Mind, Change Your Brain: How a New Science Reveals Our Extraordinary Potential to Transform Ourselves.* New York: Ballantine, 2008.

Bolstad, Richard, and Margot Hamblett. *Transforming Communication: Leading-Edge Professional and Personal Skills.* Auckland: Longman, 1997.

Bolton, Robert. "Listening Is More Than Merely Hearing." In *Bridges Not Walls: A Book about Interpersonal Communication*, edited by John Stewart, 175–92. New York: McGraw-Hill, 1990.

Bonhoeffer, Dietrich. *Life Together.* London: SCM, 1967.

Brown, Brené. "Brené Brown on Empathy vs Sympathy [*sic*]." YouTube video, 2:53. Uploaded by "Diana Simon Psihoterapeut," April 1, 2016. https://tinyurl.com/y8u3gvvg.

———. *Daring Greatly: How the Courage to Be Vulnerable Transforms the Way We Live, Love, Parent, and Lead.* New York: Gotham, 2012.

Buechner, Frederick. *Wishful Thinking: A Seeker's ABC.* San Francisco: HarperSanFrancisco, 1993.

Burnett, David. *Clash of Worlds: What Christians Can Do in a World of Cultures in Conflict.* London: Monarch, 2002.

Calhoun, Adele Ahlberg. *Spiritual Disciplines Handbook: Practices That Transform Us.* Downers Grove, IL: InterVarsity, 2005.

Campbell, Alistair V. *Professionalism and Pastoral Care.* Edited by Don S. Browning. Philadelphia: Fortress Press, 1985.

Carlozzi, Barbara L., Carrie Winterowd, R. Stephen Harrist, Nancy Thomason, Kristi Bratkovich, and Sheri Worth. "Spirituality, Anger, and Stress in Early Adolescence." *Journal of Religion and Health* 49, no. 4 (2010): 445–59.

Chaplin, Jonathan. *Multiculturalism: A Christian Retrieval.* London: Theos, 2011.

Christerson, Brad, and Michael Emerson. "The Costs of Diversity in Religious Organizations: An In-Depth Case Study." *Sociology of Religion* 64, no. 2 (2003): 163–82.

Clebsch, William A., and Charles R. Jaekle. *Pastoral Care in Historical Perspective*. New York: Harper & Row, 1967.

Cole, Allan Hugh. "What Makes Care Pastoral?" *Pastoral Psychology* 59, no. 6 (2010): 711–23.

Conde-Frazier, Elizabeth, S. Steve Hang, and Gary A. Parrett, eds. *A Many Colored Kingdom: Multicultural Dynamics for Spiritual Formation*. Grand Rapids: Baker, 2004.

Cooper-White, Pamela. *Shared Wisdom: Use of the Self in Pastoral Care and Counseling*. Minneapolis: Fortress Press, 2004.

Covert, Henry G. *Ministry to the Incarcerated*. Chicago: Loyola University Press, 1995.

DeVito, Joseph, Susan O'Rourke, and Linda O'Neill. *Human Communication*. New Zealand edition. Auckland: Longman, 2000.

DeYmaz, Mark, and Harry Li. *Ethnic Blends: Mixing Diversity into Your Local Church*. Grand Rapids: Zondervan, 2010.

Dimbleby, Richard, and Graeme Burton. *More Than Words: An Introduction to Communication*. 4th ed. London: Routledge, 2007.

Doehring, Carrie. *The Practice of Pastoral Care: A Postmodern Approach*. Louisville: Westminster John Knox, 2015.

Dwyer, Jeffrey W., Gary R. Lee, and Thomas B. Jankowski. "Reciprocity, Elder Satisfaction, and Caregiver Stress and Burden: The Exchange of Aid in the Family Caregiving Relationship." *Journal of Marriage and the Family* 56, no. 1 (February 1994): 35–43.

Dykstra, Robert C., ed. *Images of Pastoral Care*. St. Louis, MO: Chalice, 2005.

Eck, Diana L. "Is Our God Listening? Exclusivism, Inclusivism, and Pluralism." In *Islam and Global Dialogue: Religious Pluralism and the Pursuit of Peace*, edited by Roger Boase, 21–49. Aldershot: Ashgate, 2005.

Epel, Elissa S., Rachel Lapidus, Bruce McEwen, and Kelly Brownell. "Stress May Add Bite to Appetite in Women: A Laboratory Study of Stress-Induced Cortisol and Eating Behavior." *Psychoneuroendocrinology* 26, no. 1 (2001): 37–49.

Epel, Elissa S., Bruce McEwen, Teresa Seeman, Karen Matthews, Grace Castellazzo, Kelly D. Brownell, Jennifer Bell, and Jeannette R. Ickovics. "Stress and Body Shape: Stress-Induced Cortisol Secretion Is Consistently Greater among Women with Central Fat." *Psychosomatic Medicine* 62, no. 5 (2000): 623–32.

Evans, Pamela. *The Overcommitted Christian: Serving God without Wearing Out*. Downers Grove, IL: InterVarsity, 2001.

Faller, George R., and Heather Wright. *Sacred Stress: A Radically Different Approach to Using Life's Challenges for Positive Change*. Woodstock, VT: Skylight Paths, 2016.

Farabaugh, Tim. *Lay Pastoral Care Giving*. Nashville: Discipleship Resources, 2009.

Forman, Daniel E., Aaron D. Berman, Carolyn H. McCabe, Donald S. Baim, and Jeanne Y. Wei. "PTCA in the Elderly: The 'Young-Old' versus the 'Old-Old.'" *Journal of the American Geriatrics Society* 40, no. 1 (1992): 19–22.

Foster, Richard J. *A Celebration of Discipline: The Path to Spiritual Growth*. San Francisco: Harper & Row, 1978.

Foster, Richard J., and Gayle D. Beebe. *Longing for God: Seven Paths of Christian Devotion*. Downers Grove, IL: InterVarsity, 2009.

Foster, Richard J., and Kathryn A. Yanni. *Celebrating the Disciplines: A Journal Workbook to Accompany Celebration of Discipline*. San Francisco: HarperSanFrancisco, 1992.

Fowler, Gene. "The Ministry of Pastoral Care in Twenty-First-Century Protestant Congregations." *Pastoral Psychology* 61, no. 2 (2012): 197–210.

Gerkin, Charles V. *An Introduction to Pastoral Care*. Nashville: Abingdon, 1997.

Graham, Elaine L. *Transforming Practice: Pastoral Theology in an Age of Uncertainty*. Eugene, OR: Wipf & Stock, 2002.

Green, Joel B. "Caring as Gift and Goal: Biblical and Theological Reflections." In *The Crisis of Care: Affirming and Restoring Caring Practices in the Helping Professions*, edited by Susan S. Phillips and Patricia Benner, 149–67. Washington, DC: Georgetown University Press, 1994.

Grenz, Stanley J. *Created for Community: Connecting Christian Belief with Christian Living*. Wheaton, IL: Victor Books, 1996.

———. *The Social God and the Relational Self: A Trinitarian Theology of the Imago Dei*. Louisville: Westminster John Knox, 2001.

Groody, Daniel G. "Crossing the Divide: Foundations of a Theology of Migration." *Theological Studies* 70, no. 3 (2009): 638–67.

———. "Theology in the Age of Migration: Seeing the Image of Christ in the Eyes of a Stranger." *National Catholic Reporter*, September 14, 2009. https://tinyurl.com/y73eqyxk.

Gulley, Philip. "Why I Am a Progressive Christian." *Grace Talks* (blog). https://tinyurl.com/ycb2jwvs.

Hammond, Kim, and Darren Cronshaw. *Sentness: Six Postures of Missional Christians*. Downers Grove, IL: InterVarsity, 2014.

Harris, Paula, and Doug Schaupp. *Being White: Finding Our Place in a Multiethnic World*. Downers Grove, IL: InterVarsity, 2004.

Hartwig, Ryan T., and Warren Bird. *Teams That Thrive: Five Disciplines of Collaborative Church Leadership.* Downers Grove, IL: InterVarsity, 2015.

Hicks, Douglas A., and Mark R. Valeri. *Global Neighbors: Christian Faith and Moral Obligation in Today's Economy.* Grand Rapids: Eerdmans, 2008.

Hill, Graham. *Salt, Light, and a City: Introducing Missional Ecclesiology.* Eugene, OR: Wipf & Stock, 2012.

Hill, Reuben. "Generic Features of Families Under Stress." *Social Casework* 49, no. 2 (1958): 139–50.

Hirsch, Alan. "Defining Missional." *Christianity Today.* Fall 2008. https://tinyurl.com/yct3z8lc.

Hobbes, Michael. "America Already Has Extreme Vetting." *Rottin' in Denmark* (blog). February 15, 2017. https://tinyurl.com /ycudswos.

———. "How Mark Zuckerberg Should Give Away $45 Billion." *Huffington Post.* February 24, 2016. https://tinyurl.com /yax4z7hf.

———. "Stop Trying to Save the World." *The New Republic.* November 17, 2014. https://tinyurl.com/hthj9zw.

Holm, Neil. "Toward a Theology of the Ministry of Presence in Chaplaincy." *Journal of Christian Education* 52, no. 1 (May 2009): 7–22.

Holmes, Thomas H., and Richard H. Rahe. "The Social Readjustment Rating Scale." *Journal of Psychosomatic Research* 11, no. 2 (1967): 213–18.

Hunter, Rodney J. *Dictionary of Pastoral Care and Counseling.* 3rd ed. Nashville: Abingdon, 1990.

Jackson, Craig A. "The Life Events Inventory (LEI)." *Occupational Medicine* 59, no. 3 (2009): 208.

Jensma, Jeanne L. "Critical Incident Intervention with Missionaries." *Journal of Psychology and Theology* 27, no. 2 (1999): 130–38.

Johnson, Lydia F. *Drinking from the Same Well: Cross-Cultural Concerns in Pastoral Care and Counseling*. Eugene, OR: Pickwick, 2011.

Jones, Tony. *The Sacred Way: Spiritual Practices for Everyday Life*. Grand Rapids: Zondervan, 2005.

Kanner, Allen D., James C. Coyne, Catherine Schaefer, and Richard S. Lazarus. "Comparison of Two Modes of Stress Measurement: Daily Hassles and Uplifts versus Major Life Events." *Journal of Behavioral Medicine* 4, no. 1 (1981): 1–39.

Kasperkevic, Jana. "Why Is America So Afraid to Take a Vacation?" *The Guardian*, September 7, 2015. https://tinyurl.com/yc5jxhzx.

Kayler, Claude J. "Clergy Stress: A Study of Stressors and Stress-Relieving Practices among United Methodist Clergy across Three Districts of the Western North Caroline Conference." Doctor of Ministry Thesis, Asbury Theological Seminary, 2011.

Keizer, Garrett. *Help: The Original Human Dilemma*. San Francisco: HarperSanFrancisco, 2004.

Klein, Sarah. "6 Surprising Causes of Inflammation—And What You Can Do about It." *Prevention*, May 14, 2015. https://tinyurl.com/yd6bn2vh.

Kriz, Tony. "Blessings of a Post-Christian Culture." *Christianity Today*, March 2015. https://tinyurl.com/ybrtrgh8.

Lartey, Emmanuel Y. "Global Views for Pastoral Care and Counseling: Postmodern, Post-Colonial, Post-Christian, Post-Human, Post-Pastoral." Address at the 7th Asia-Pacific Congress on Pastoral Care and Counseling, July 15, 2009, Perth, Australia.

———. *In Living Color: An Intercultural Approach to Pastoral Care and Counseling*. London: Jessica Kingsley, 2003.

Levitt, Peggy, and B. Nada Jaworsky. "Transnational Migration: Past Developments and Future Trends." *Annual Review of Sociology* 33, no. 1 (2007): 129–56.

Lincoln, Karen D., Linda M. Chatters, and Robert Joseph Taylor. "Social Support, Traumatic Events, and Depressive Symptoms among African Americans." *Journal of Marriage and Family* 67, no. 3 (2005): 754–66.

Maholmes, Valerie. *Fostering Resilience and Well-Being in Children and Families in Poverty: Why Hope Still Matters*. Oxford: Oxford University Press, 2014.

McClure, Barbara J. *Moving beyond Individualism in Pastoral Care and Counseling: Reflections on Theory, Theology and Practice*. Cambridge: Lutterworth, 2011.

McHugh, Adam S. *The Listening Life: Embracing Attentiveness in a World of Distraction*. Downers Grove, IL: InterVarsity, 2015.

McLendon, Russell. "11 Alarming Facts about Sea Level Rise." Mother Nature Network. February 26, 2016. https://tinyurl .com/ybon3njx.

McLeod, Saul. "Stress and Life Events." *Simply Psychology*, 2010. https://tinyurl.com/ydavmca5.

McNeil, Brenda Salter, and Rick Richardson. *The Heart of Racial Justice: How Soul Change Leads to Social Change*. Downers Grove, IL: InterVarsity, 2004.

Miller-McLemore, Bonnie J. "The Human Web: Reflections on the State of Pastoral Theology." *Christian Century*, April 7, 1993, 366–69.

Minirth, Frank, Paul Meier, Don Hawkins, Chris Thurmon, and
Rich Flournoy. *Beating Burnout: Balanced Living for Busy People.*
New York: Inspirational Press, 1997.

Ministry of Pacific Island Affairs. "Demographic Fact Sheet."
https://tinyurl.com/yddy6mgx.

New York Times. "Rev. Seward Hiltner, 74, Dies; Taught at Princeton
Seminary." November 28, 1984. https://tinyurl.com/y9y6e6ob.

Nouwen, Henri. "Care." *Cornerstone* 26, no. 11 (1997): 8.

———. *Life of the Beloved: Spiritual Living in a Secular World.* New
York: Crossroad, 1992.

———. "Moving from Solitude to Community to Ministry."
Leadership 16, no. 2 (Spring 1995): 81–87.

———. *The Wounded Healer: Ministry in Contemporary Society.* New
York: Doubleday, 1979.

Noyce, Gaylord B. "Has Ministry's Nerve Been Cut by the Pastoral
Counseling Movement?" *Christian Century*, February 1, 1978,
103–6.

Oates, Wayne E. *Grief, Transition, and Loss: A Pastor's Practical Guide.*
Minneapolis: Fortress Press, 1997.

Oden, Amy G. *And You Welcomed Me: A Sourcebook on Hospitality in
Early Christianity.* Nashville: Abingdon, 2001.

OECD. "Foreign Born Population." https://tinyurl.com/y87b6ezf.

Oswald, Roy M. *Clergy Self-Care: Finding a Balance for Effective
Ministry.* Washington, DC: Alban Institute, 1991.

Ovans, Andrea. "What Resilience Means, and Why It Matters."
Harvard Business Review, January 5, 2015. https://tinyurl.com
/nf9zrcu.

Patterson, Joan M. "Understanding Family Resilience." *Journal of Clinical Psychology* 58, no. 3 (2002): 233–46.

Pattison, Stephen. *A Critique of Pastoral Care.* London: SCM, 2000.

Patton, John. *Pastoral Care: An Essential Guide.* Nashville: Abingdon, 2005.

Pearson, David. "Crossing Ethnic Thresholds: Multiculturalisms in Comparative Perspectives." In *Nga Patai: Racism and Ethnic Relations in Aotearoa New Zealand*, edited by Paul Spoonley, David Pearson, and Cluny Macpherson, 247–95. Palmerston North, NZ: Dunmore, 1996.

Peterson, Eugene H. "Curing Souls: The Forgotten Art." *Christianity Today*, Summer 1983, https://tinyurl.com/ybckrpeq.

Phillips, Katherine W. "How Diversity Works." *Scientific American* 311, no. 4 (October 2014): 31–35.

Pohl, Christine D. "A Community's Practice of Hospitality: The Interdependence of Practices and of Communities." In *Practicing Theology: Beliefs and Practices in Christian Life*, edited by Miroslav Volf and Dorothy C. Bass, 121–36. Grand Rapids: Eerdmans, 2002.

———. *Making Room: Recovering Hospitality as a Christian Tradition.* Grand Rapids: Eerdmans, 1999.

Postema, Don. *Catch Your Breath: God's Invitation to Sabbath Rest.* Grand Rapids: CRC Press, 1997.

Purves, Andrew. *Pastoral Theology in the Classical Tradition.* Louisville: Westminster John Knox, 2001.

Rah, Soong-Chan. *Many Colors: Cultural Intelligence for a Changing Church.* Chicago: Moody, 2010.

"Report of the World Council of Churches Consultation on Mission and Ecclesiology of the Migrant Churches." *International Review of Missions* 100, no. 1 (April 2011): 104–7.

Rhodes, Stephen A. *Where the Nations Meet: The Church in a Multicultural World*. Downers Grove, IL: InterVarsity, 1998.

Rohr, Richard. *Breathing Under Water: Spirituality and the Twelve Steps*. Cincinnati, OH: St. Anthony Messenger Press, 2011.

Roxburgh, Alan. *Joining God, Remaking the Church, Changing the World: The New Shape of the Church in Our Time*. New York: Morehouse, 2015.

Roxburgh, Alan, and Fred Romanuk. *The Missional Leader: Equipping Your Church to Meet a Changing World*. San Francisco: Jossey-Bass, 2006.

Sanchez, Mariana, Frank R. Dillon, Maritza Concha, and Mario De La Rosa. "The Impact of Religious Coping on the Acculturative Stress and Alcohol Use of Recent Latino Immigrants." *Journal of Religion and Health* 54, no. 6 (2015): 1986–2004.

Sanford, John A. *Ministry Burnout*. Louisville: Westminster John Knox, 1982.

Satterlee, Craig. "Holy and Active Listening." Alban Institute. https://tinyurl.com/y7n5tsxb. Adapted from *When God Speaks through Change: Preaching in Times of Congregational Transition*. Herndon, VA: Alban Institute, 2005.

Sparks, Paul, Tim Soerens, and Dwight J. Friesen. *The New Parish: How Neighborhood Churches Are Transforming Mission, Discipleship and Community*. Downers Grove, IL: InterVarsity, 2014.

Statistics New Zealand. "2013 Census Quick Stats about Culture and Identity." April 15, 2014. https://tinyurl.com/y7yb2bat.

———. "2013 Census Quick Stats about Māori." December 3, 2013. https://tinyurl.com/y9m5nqf3.

Stone, Howard W. "The Congregational Setting of Pastoral Counseling: A Study of Pastoral Counseling Theorists from 1949–1999." *Journal of Pastoral Care* 55, no. 2 (2001): 181–96.

———. *Theological Context for Pastoral Caregiving: Word in Deed.* London: Routledge, 1996.

Swenson, Richard A. *Margin: Restoring Emotional, Physical, Financial, and Time Reserves to Overloaded Lives.* Colorado Springs: NavPress, 1992.

Thompson, Marjorie J. *Soul Feast: An Invitation to the Christian Spiritual Life.* Louisville: Westminster John Knox, 1995.

van Beek, Aart M. "A Cross-Cultural Case for Convergence in Pastoral Thinking and Training." *Pastoral Psychology* 59, no. 4 (2010): 471–81.

Verderber, Kathleen S., and Rudolph F. Verderber. *Inter-Act: Interpersonal Communication Concepts, Skills, and Contexts.* 10th ed. New York: Oxford University Press, 2004.

Ward, Kevin R. *Losing Our Religion: Changing Patterns of Believing and Belonging in Secular Western Societies.* Eugene, OR: Wipf & Stock, 2013.

Way, Peggy. *Created by God: Pastoral Care for All God's People.* St. Louis, MO: Chalice, 2005.

Weems, Lovett H., Jr. *Church Leadership: Vision, Team, Culture, Integrity.* Nashville: Abingdon, 2010.

Wilmoth, Joe D., and Samantha Smyser. "The ABC-X Model of Family Stress in the Book of Philippians." *Journal of Psychology and Theology* 37, no. 3 (2009): 155–62.

Wimberly, John W., Jr. *Mobilizing Congregations: How Teams Can Motivate Members and Get Things Done.* Lanham, MD: Rowman & Littlefield, 2015.

Wingate, Andrew. "Mission as Dialogue: A Contextual Study from Leicester, UK." In *The Gospel among Religions: Christian Ministry, Theology, and Spirituality in a Multifaith World*, edited by David R. Brockman and Ruben L. F. Habito, 153–67. Maryknoll, NY: Orbis, 2010.

Zimmer, Carl. "Genes for Skin Color Rebut Dated Notions of Race, Researchers Say." *New York Times*, October 12, 2017. https://tinyurl.com/y9ns8zb6.